Not Over Yet

simple

strategies

to struggle

less and

savor more

Aruni Nan Futuronsky

First published by Dog Ear Publishing
4010 W. 86th Street, Ste H
Indianapolis, IN 46268
www.dogearpublishing.net

ISBN: 978-1-4575-2356-4

This paper is printed on acid free paper.
Printed in the United States of America

gratitude and appreciation

For everything.

For everyone.

Eventually.

Contents

Author's Note

This book is a work of creative non-fiction. My intention has been to protect the privacy of all the people who have blessed my life while also portraying it accurately. Some characters are composites and certain timelines have been altered. The events described are filtered through the lens of time, space, and those funny tricks memory sometimes plays. I offer them to you as an honest reflection of my experiences.

Introduction

Someone recently asked me which teachers inspire me. The more I thought about the question, the more surprised I was by my response. I learn from reality, my greatest guru, my most profound teacher, the partner that continues to evolve me forward into the world. I learn from the people who sit in front of me in classes, from the people I meet during my day, from the circumstances I am given. Life gives me what I need to grow. Of that, I am positive. And as I live within this paradigm, I can no longer comfortably be a victim, shaking my fist against the heavens proclaiming, "Bastards!"—a favorite oldie-but-goodie mantra of mine.

If life is coming to heal me, to give me what I need to become more of who I really am, no matter the circumstances that lesson is wrapped in, no matter the feelings it evokes, It (whatever the It is of the moment: a challenge at work, a family member with a medical difficulty, insecurity about the future and finances, fill in the blank) is a gift. It is a gift. And from that gift, seeds of my future blossoming lie. As I move away from the victim role, I am freed up to grow and learn and evolve. And I struggle less!

Hence, this book. I wanted to write a book that offered some of the current experiences that have acted as my teachers and my guides, along with some strategies to get the most juice, the most guts, the most bang for our *kishkas* (Yiddish word for innards—sorry, I was compelled to write that), in order to move through the process.

What process, you might ask? The process of integration, of moving through the body/mind, the feelings and thoughts that life triggers. Life's job is to trigger responses in us, to offer us opportunities to feel and release the old, stuck feelings and patterns in our body/mind. Call it integration, transmutation, transformation—it works. We feel, we relax, we let the feelings move through, and we are freer.

As we struggle against the feelings that life's circumstances invoke, we suffer. Just like yoga on the mat, as we relax around the sensations that life in its perfection evokes, both on and off the mat, transmutation happens sooner and easier. As we struggle against reality, we miss the glory, the beauty—of the soft, pink, misty sunrise, of the dog walking down the street calmly carrying that giant log, the light on the trees in the late afternoon. Struggling against life sucks us dry of life energy and absents us from its beauty and grace of the moment.

Oh, and most importantly, this paradigm is not about denying feelings, a process I fondly call premature transcendence. It is not, "Oh, I have a feeling. I'm angry. I surrender." To the contrary. This journey of wholeness is through the feelings, allowing them to act as doorways to deeper integration. Almost counter-intuitively, the way out is through.

It's not the feelings that hurt us; it is what we do to try to control and resist and modify those feelings that brings suffering.

Okay. Enough. Now:

Let me tell you about this out-of-the-box book you are holding. This book is a co-creation, between me and you. Bring a pen to it; bring your favorite markers or some crayons. Bring yourself to it and let's interactively flesh out this roadmap together for this next phase of your evolution.

Each chapter is composed of one of twelve narratives, twelve stories of situations, places, and challenges that have touched me and grown me. I have been committed to preserving the narratives of my life; their richness, synchronicity, and simplicity amaze me. Read them. Enjoy them or not. See what they touch in you. Find your own teachings and guidance in them, as I did.

The narratives begin and end with quotes that have touched me over the years of my practice, quotes that I hope resonate in tone and theme with each of the specific chapters.

And then, I have offered you strategies. Following each narrative and its ending quote, you will find two additional sections. The first is called "*Questions for Your Heart*." The second is called "*Practice for Your Life*."

Questions for Your Heart have the function, like a doorway, to open your own relationship to the teachings, reflecting for you where they resonate in your particular life moment. I offer them with all humility to your heart, not so much to your brain. We all know your brain is brilliant—I imagine that it's just a tad in the way of your healing and mindful development. Think of your mind as an overdeveloped muscle, needing relaxing. The heart, however, demands our attention and our focus for its unfoldment.

So let's relax the mind and stimulate the heart, shall we?

Revisit these ideas. Ponder them. Let them come alive in you. Utilize this interactive book like a roadmap—let it lead you forward.

The final section of each chapter, *Practice for Your Life*, is a training in repetitive reframe, prayer, or meditation, to continually stretch your muscle of mindfulness. Let them touch you—return to them, as your heart feels so called. I offer them to your heart as a rite of evolution.

Enough said. In those fabulous Twelve Step words, "Take what you like and leave the rest." My hope is that there is one kernel, one seed, one idea that can be planted deep inside your heart, to blossom into your next flowering up ahead.

Let's relax into the journey together.

1

Permission to Practice

The highest spiritual practice is self-observation without judgment.
—Swami Kripalu

This is a story about dogs—and so much more. Dog stories and dogs themselves tend to be about so much more than just dogs.

I heard someone once say that we are divine beings, learning how to be human. I've pondered that one for a long time. This is what I have discovered: Left to my own human devices, I am a nut. My tendency is to imagine the worst about myself and about life around me. However, I choose to not live like that. So I practice.

I practice managing my human fear. I practice believing in the best about the people around me. I practice speaking my truth and letting go of the results. And I fall off the metaphoric yoga mat of practice all the time. Like the Buddhists say, if you fall down eighty-four times, get up eighty-five.

Whenever I notice my behavior, I take a breath, I bless that human part of me, and I realign to how I want to live.

I get up.

The time in question, this dog-related tumble off the mat, was quite emotionally catastrophic. I didn't just fall—I plummeted, plunged, and wildly tumbled, losing all foot-hold to perspective and trust. The good news in this tale is that I found my way back to emotional balance relatively quickly. But, in this breach, I endured much self-inflicted pain and struggle.

The canine connection, my dogs, Lucy Doodle and Zac Joseph Doodle, are constant gifts of love and growth for me. In their fuzzy, larger-than-life Muppet-ness, they bring me such lessons. They are shiny mirrors into which I see my behavior, recognize my strengths and growth, and see beyond my old patterns of limited thinking. Simply put, my dogs are my teachers. They grow me.

Whenever one of them is at risk physically, I have the opportunity to embody my practice and outlive my fear. Zac is a strong, young, and wildly accident-prone fellow, while Lucy is older, and more willing to eat the delicious inedibles she finds everywhere, like the delicious plastic Starbucks coffee lid discarded at the side of the path or the yummy tube sock awaiting her in the woods. I have had plenty of opportunities to take action and let go of the results—thanks to my dogs.

One of the more exciting recent culinary experiments was undertaken, we believe, by a Lucy-and-Zac partnership. Together they managed to extricate Aunt Mary's vitamin case from her bag on the table, chew it open, and gorge themselves on huge amounts of mega-vitamins, chasing the whole combination down with yummy bites of Klonopin, her prescription anti-anxiety medication. After a long and heart-wrenching discussion with the National Poison Control people, with wild calculations of potential dog doses of things (thank goodness for Aunt Mary's Type A vitamin and supplement list), the canines were deemed fine. They both appeared quite relaxed by the end of the evening. The humans on the scene, Ras and Aunt Mary, on the other hand, were neither fine nor relaxed. I was fortunate enough to learn about the day's events *after* the potentially gruesome incident, when all the players were comfortably resting.

But it is of another experience I wish to speak, one that offered more emotional learning for me. I fell off the wagon hard with this one last week, in spite of knowing that living in the moment is the surest antidote to my catapulting fear.

It started with an innocent-enough little lump in Lucy's ear. A trip to our calm and New-Age-ish vet, Dr. T., for assurance ended with our normally placid doc avoiding my eyes, as she strained to look inside Lucy's ear. Was she really avoiding my eyes? Or was my mind . . . ?

Her voice was taut with seriousness: "This growth is pink AND raised. We must get it out for a biopsy as soon as possible."

I got stuck on the *pink AND raised* part of her comment.

"Would it be better if it was either pink *or* raised?" I asked some-what ridiculously, tap-dancing around the depth of my fear.

Eyebrow raised, she shot me an incredulous look.

"Let's schedule a time in the next few days that I can take it out," was her answer, ignoring my deflecting question.

I don't know what happened. A surge of fear took over like a tsu-nami inside my belly. I know that my fear is a harbinger, signaling that useless thoughts and self-centered distortions are a'coming. Much of the time I am able to notice the fear, honor it, and begin dismantling it. Much of the time.

But not this time. Perhaps because I was tired, or because of our upcoming vacation, or because of the physical reminders of Zac's recent brush with death (yes, death), I was defenseless.

My fear became reality.

My mind took charge: never a good turn of events.

The next twenty-four hours were a blur of worst-case scenarios playing out in the manic movie-theater of my brain. Nightmarish thoughts controlled me. But what about the vacation we were going on next week? What about my wife's birthday celebration? How do you celebrate with a dying dog next to you?

Yes, I did envision poor Lucy dying at my side.

Sleep that night was a hellish journey. At 2:00 AM, lying in bed, I found myself planning her funeral, despite her very alive and adorable snoring on the floor next to me. By 3:00 AM, in a burst of positivity, I saw myself scheduling chemotherapy appointments for her at the famous vet hospital in Boston. By 5:00 AM, I was bleary, shaky with worry, and feeling good for nobody/nothing.

The day dawned, in spite of me. As I stumbled toward the mirror, I saw who was looking back at me—a haggard woman, baggy-eyed and pale, believing the worst about life. In that moment, I made a decision: I would practice believing the best about life, about me, about Lucy, about us, all. I would get back on the mat—that damn mat—of my practice, trusting and partnering with life. I would practice being in this moment, just this single moment, which life gave me.

The moments ahead, no matter what they might bring, would unfold. They would take care of themselves. This moment was all that I had.

Resolved, I rigorously immersed myself into my morning activities that strengthen the quieting of my mind, typically overcompensating yet righteously focused: a thirty-five-minute dog walk with prayer and mantra, followed by my delicious yet slightly wacky-minded meditation practice. Off to work with mantra on my lips, recognizing the fear as it seeped toward me, warding it away with an amended prayer of surrender from my Twelve Step program:

> "I offer Lucy Doodle to You, to build her and to make of her as you choose."

I repeated this prayer 1,936 times that day.

And the day unfolded. And some tentative balance was reestablished. I managed to show up for my work responsibilities, teaching and coaching, with some semblance of presence. Perhaps I was holding a tad too tightly onto this balance, but holding nevertheless.

So twenty-four hours later, when Dr. T's cheerful voice proclaimed on the phone, "It's benign," I was able to put down the phone, sob for five straight minutes, and go home—to walk the dogs, my teachers and guides who bring me life, to pack for the vacation, and to get over myself.

Is there a moral to this story?

Reality, in its relentlessness, will unfold however it does. As I am willing and able to stay in the moment with reality, no matter what it brings me, it all becomes manageable. As I leap ahead, drawing my own (usually worst-case) conclusions about what is up ahead, I lose a profound partner. Call it Life, call it Grace, call it God, call it the Moment, call it Nothing—when I hop ahead and take over the show, I am alone and oh, so terribly unprepared to manage the entire universe. I do it really badly.

When I stay here, in this moment, when I give myself permission to practice, I am freed.

Walking Lucy and Zac down our little dirt road in the soft afternoon light, I chuckle at my own forgetfulness. Forgetting and falling off the mat is part of the process, for certain. One can't remember without forgetting—and what is forgetting, but another opportunity to remember more authentically?

But staying on the mat is surely more comfortable.

I will continue to practice. Life is just easier that way.

Whatever is occurring in the present moment is what we need to deal with right now. Staying with our real experience of ourselves and our situation will teach us exactly what we need to know for growth.
—The Wisdom of the Enneagram, p. 346

Questions for Your Heart

- As you practice observing your thoughts without judgment, what do you notice?
- How do feelings occur in your body? Do you get hot? Sweaty? Tight? Just notice.
- How do you escape your feelings? Observe your own MO.
- Name some of the thoughts/beliefs that scare you about feeling what's occurring in your moment.

 ## Practice for Your Life

Observe yourself today with radical compassion. As you notice your thoughts and your behavior veering away from how you choose to live, take a breath. Bless that part of yourself. Realign with your intention through right action. Keep it simple—remember, give yourself full permission to practice.

2

That Time of Year . . .
On the Taconic Parkway

Long ago, it must be, I have a photograph
Preserve your memories, they're all that's left you
—Paul Simon

The rain seemed never-ending, filling up the entire day that Witchie died and leaking into the next, our travel day. It came down in straight sheets, the heavens seeming to open up and saturate the core of the earth. And with it came our tears.

We packed the car cautiously, dodging the rain as best we could, raincoats heavy on our bodies in their wet clinginess. Careful with each other now and moving with self-conscious prudence, we joined our energies for this joint endeavor, something we have historically done so well. We have always worked well together, rallying around an external task with wordless fluidity. Whether it's setting up a tent in a windstorm, teaching a group of diverse people, or focusing on an annoying cleaning project in the house, we come together well. This has always been our strength.

And it is a strength we have so needed these past months, and a strength that has, to some degree, evaded us, too.

Suitcases flung into the hatchback, we evaded the puddles and hopped into the car, shaking off the clinging rain. We looked at each other, smiled carefully, and headed the car toward New Jersey, toward my sister's house.

Several overwhelming challenges befell us this spring into summer, now landing us into this tentative moment of mid-October. Ras, my wife, struggling with some untraceable digestive challenges, continued to lose weight, leaving her at an emaciated and gaunt eighty-seven pounds. Watching her waste away, acknowledging my helplessness in the process, unfortunately did not spur me to my higher relational self. My fear morphed into a distancing, a pulling away of my heart; my support became external, focused on over-involvement in her food intake, missing the emotional window available to both of us to get closer. It was a time of unacknowledged terror, triggering in me the ancient and endless illnesses of my dead father. I watched her energy drain, while feeling the energy in our marriage also dissipating.

I was not proud of my limited capacities, yet I felt powerless over them, cause for more frustration. No leverage seemed to exist for me to shift gears, to climb through my gnawing worry to get closer to my ailing partner's heart. I was just too scared.

And in the midst of this, Witchie, dear Witchie, Ras's half-sister, surrogate-mother, friend, mentor—a truly bigger-than-life being—began her slow decline through the end of her life. At eighty-eight, she was tired and ready to go. This tripod-process felt crazy-making and endless to me; Ras, wasting away in front of me, Witchie, in her parallel wasting, far away in Wisconsin, and our marriage stalling and stumbling along. It was an untenable, heavy and incessant time, spring into summer, dry and hollow, and culminating now in this last breath of a gloriously colorful autumn.

Like with all things, time takes time.

Witchie continued sliding further and further inside herself. Taken first from her was movement, then speech, then hunger, her huge eyes reflecting loss after loss. Then, of course, the final loss, the giving up of her life, last evening, a still October night, her children sitting with her, Ras hundreds of miles away lying next to me in bed.

Ras's process, too, had shifted. Her weight loss finally had creaked to a stop around the summer's end. She began slowly gaining ground and weight, inching her way back toward this, the new normal.

Some energy seemed to return to our marriage, too. My renewing a therapeutic relationship helped me to begin to see through my denial into my terror of losing my wife and began to reestablish in me some tools for jump-starting connection between us.

It was a new moment.

The frustrations and the fears of the past months were quieter now; Witchie had died, the inevitable had finally and actually happened. Ras would leave next week for Wisconsin and the memorial. However, for this weekend, we had committed to see my sister and her family in New Jersey. We decided to go anyway. Although I still wanted to run alone in a thousand diverse directions, screeching my feelings to the planets, I shifted the car into reverse and backed out of the driveway, leaving our house and the Doodles, their dog-sitter coming later, behind us.

We were traveling together again. It felt like a long time since we had. We wove our way through the back roads, heading toward the Thruway which would snake us south to Jersey, speaking of Witchie in quiet voices, speaking softly of things passed. Somewhere inside of me I felt a shift of breath, a collapsing of a barrier of some sort.

We were gentle and soft with each other.

About thirty minutes into the journey I looked up, looked around, and saw the road with new eyes:

"I'm headed toward the Taconic Parkway!" I exclaimed. "I meant to go on the Thruway. It would be better in the rain and fog."

It seemed impossible that I had made such an unconscious error. For the past years, I always traveled on the Thruway to New Jersey—it was just easier and more direct. The Taconic Parkway, in all its beauty, ambled and puttered its way south. Its winding roads would certainly be more difficult in the bad weather.

"Should I backtrack our way to the Thruway?" I asked, knowing this would add some time to our trip.

"You're driving—it's your call," was Ras's response.

For reasons I didn't understand, reasons that seemed to short-circuit my logic, I chose to keep on this route. Perhaps I lacked the energy to try to change course—it just seemed easier to carry on as we were headed. So the Taconic awaited us.

We pulled onto it a few minutes later, following its arrows to the south. It seemed we were the only car on the highway, for now at least. The road opened up before us. The rain, still constant, seemed softer, easier, almost welcoming us, encouraging us forward.

We talked ourselves into silence. The only sounds were the tires on the wet roadway, the hum of the windshield wipers, and the soft patter of rain. Ras flicked on our public radio station, knowing we would lose its coverage shortly. For now, however, they were playing a Paul Simon retrospective, playing his older, more familiar songs. Since he is one of our favorites, we settled into the quiet comfort of listening to his words, words that were so deeply planted in both of our memories and in both of our lives.

And the leaves! Oh, the leaves; yellow and golden in their aging, in their dying, they created a canopy of soft grace through which we drove. Paul Simon humming his poetry in our ears, the car softly purring forward, we moved through this glory, taking us into another dimension of softness.

Ras leaned over and took my hand. Her hand was dry and familiar, its shape fitting perfectly into mine, two pieces of the puzzle merging effortlessly together.

We drove on through this suspended grace.

Witchie died, I thought. *And Ras didn't.* We were still together, aging, getting sick, recovering, pulling farther away from each other, coming back again.

Something else deep inside me surrendered. I felt a rush of soft goodness pass through me, surrounding me, holding me in its loving arms. The quality of my breath seemed to change, as did the very air around me.

I found myself thinking, *I feel—what's the word?—remarkably wonderful. I feel a strong sense of wellness, of aliveness . . .*

But that didn't even scratch the surface of language, to convey this emotional/physical suspension I felt, this being carried forward through beauty, through time, through life, through the hard, through the death, and continuing along.

Continuing. Continuing along together.

In our aging.

In our illnesses.

In our losses.

In the hard times.

I settled into the car seat more deeply, tears in my eyes, knowing that this encounter with mortality, with impermanence, could carry me forward to a more heart-based relationship with Ras. *This is the journey*, I thought, remembering the Buddhist vow I had been practicing. *This is the deal. We are aging. We are getting sick. We will continue to age. We will continue to get sick. Everything we love will be taken from us, unavoidably, eventually.*

But not now. Not yet. Not today.

There are no mistakes, I thought. *This was the route for us to take.*

We continued driving.

That time of year thou mayst in me behold (Sonnet 73)
That time of year thou mayst in me behold
When yellow leaves, or none, or few, do hang
Upon those boughs which shake against the cold,
Bare ruined choirs, where late the sweet birds sang.
In me thou see'st the twilight of such day
As after sunset fadeth in the west;
Which by and by black night doth take away,
Death's second self, that seals up all in rest.
In me thou see'st the glowing of such fire,
That on the ashes of his youth doth lie,
As the deathbed whereon it must expire,
Consumed with that which it was nourished by.
This thou perceiv'st, which makes thy love more strong,
To love that well which thou must leave ere long.
—William Shakespeare

Questions for Your Heart

- What is life asking you to let go of? Be specific.
- What is your hope or your prayer for yourself in this area of transition and change?
- What helps you to begin to relax and surrender?
- What is one thing you can give yourself today to help you to relax and surrender?

 Practice for Your Life

Notice a place in your life that might be identified as transition, change, or loss. Breathe directly into that part of yourself.

Welcome it in. Befriend it. If you can feel it, you can heal.

3

Brian, Sandy, and Team Oak Road

We have all known the long loneliness and we have learned that the only solution is love and that love comes with community.
—Dorothy Day, *The Long Loneliness: The Autobiography of the Legendary Catholic Social Activist*

The clear blue fall day, belittling the approaching storm, emboldens me. *There is much to do,* I think, belly bubbling with busy feelings, as I carry a porch chair clanging against my shins down into the basement. I have made a beyond-comprehensive list of actions for storm readiness, giving myself full permission for hyperorganization, my acknowledged and mindful hedge against my own creeping anxiety. The whole East Coast is waiting with bated breath for the landfall of this super storm, hundreds of miles wide and roaring directly toward the New York–New Jersey coast. Trying to sort hype from reality, ancient fear from smart preparedness, I struggle to keep focused on my list.

Said List:

1. Outside Stuff—take in
2. Water—buy

3. Batteries—get a thousand
4. Basement—make ready
5. Generator—befriend
6. Ditch—clean out. Damn it.

I have been doggedly working away at items 1–5 over the morning. Number 6, the dreaded ditch, hovers on the horizon.

The predictions are dire, as the superstorm approaches NYC and NJ, where my family lives. Ras—away at Witchie, dear Witchie's memorial—is a quietly encouraging yet remote voice on the phone: "It'll be fine, you'll be fine." Yet her voice echoes with a tinny distance.

It's me and the Doodles, I think. Memories of last year's storm, the water rushing down the dirt road toward our little house, continually tries to seep back into my brain. I breathe and will them away.

The morning unfolds with focused determination.

Taking a midday break at the island in our kitchen, I sip on coconut water, perusing my list. Outside stuff, now inside. *Done*, as I check it off the list. Basement, pretty ready, books moved away from windows, important things placed higher. *Done*. Water and batteries, purchased. *Done*. The generator and I are now one. *Now let's hope it keeps the sump pump pumping*, I think. Another *done*.

Looks like I am down to DITCH. The dreaded ditch from hell.

My physical projects around the house have lessened, with mowing season behind me. I have not historically been successful with longer physical projects. I'm more a get-in-there-and-get-it-done-and-go-to-the-movies type. I know full well the ditch will not allow that habitual way of being.

I head outside reluctantly. The beautiful day greets me mildly, softening against my skin like a reassuring embrace. I try to relax.

The rake's handle is thick and strangely comforting in my hands. I roll it from palm to palm, befriending it, as I peer down Oak Road. About two city blocks long with two other houses on it, it stretches before me. It's been a completely functional dirt road until the town did some "upgrades" on our sewage system, which seemed to have mysteriously disturbed the road's drainage. Since then, even a normal rainstorm sends water flowing toward our property. Our initially mindful communications to Town Hall morphed into more hysterical pleas over time. They stirred only ineffective actions from our one-man Road and Maintenance department. To date, we have another newly dug, leaf-clogged ditch to the left side of the road, as attempted support for better drainage.

My mission, should I accept it, is to rake out the ditch.

I begin. Sturdy thick-handled red rake in hand, I start across from our house, with Lucy and Zac the Dogs frolicking behind me in the yard.

Reach, rake, pull.

Reach, rake, pull.

Oh, that's not too bad, I think. Creating a pile of wet, soggy leaves in the middle of the road. Hum. *What do I think about now? Just be in the moment?*

Reach, rake, pull.

Reach, rake, pull.

My mantra emerges.

This is not a flimsy little rake, like the rakes of my childhood, with those silly, easily twisted metal teeth. No, this is a serious tool, with big chunky prongs that gather up the leaves, biting into the wet piles ruthlessly.

Behind me Lucy chases Zac madly around the apple tree, their ancient game both endlessly adorable to the people and forever appealing to the canines. *They are not abandoning the property for higher ground,* I think, *not intuitively reacting to the oncoming hurricane. Good.*

Reach, rake, pull. Reach, rake, pull. I wish I could abandon the property for higher ground. But I wouldn't leave the dogs—nor would I leave the house. With Ras away . . .

Reach, rake, pull.

I inch my way down our property, leaving larger and larger deposits of leaves mid-road. I wonder, *Is that a problem to leave them there?*

Reach, rake, pull. I feel my back. *It's okay,* I think, *to feel one's back.*

Right? Or is it a problem?

I feel sweat dripping down my spinal cord. *Fine,* I think. *Sweat is good. God made sweat.*

The leaves seem to get denser and muddier as I snake down the road. I make my way to Brian's house, our nearest neighbor, scooping out the ditch as I go.

Reach, rake, pull.

Brian is a local guy, a motorcycle-riding, EMT-working, divorced guy with a beer belly, bald head, quiet demeanor, and shy eyes.

When his young wife and daughter left a few years ago, we were somewhat horrified. Who would he be, this leather-jacketed fellow, as a single neighbor? How would he respond to us, his lesbian neighbors, without Sarah, his wife, to keep him moderated?

His boy-toys began to clog his yard: medium-sized yellow motorboat, fancy riding lawnmower, various and sundry pieces of electrical equipment, and a structure we were finally able to identify as an aluminum ice fishing hut, along with different carrying devices to motorize the above toys. His pleasures strewn around him and expanded as he claimed his singlehood.

We outlived his various home improvement projects: the painting of his house, the lawn filled with sawhorses, planks of wood. And through it all, he emerged a kind, decent, and vulnerable man, more than willing to help us. Pulling me and the Forrester out of the snowy ditch, helping to hook up the perpetually leaky hose, re-covering our tattered tent garage, waiting with us for the State Police the day our house got broken into—he has proven himself a good man. After the State Police left that night, Brian spent an hour jerry-rigging our doorframe back into shape, hammering us in safely for the night. The next day he and his friend went to Home Depot, bought a door, and spent the afternoon installing it, kindness heaped upon kindness in our time of utmost vulnerability.

Nevertheless, in spite of all his quiet goodness, I still feel shyly tentative around him, he who comes from such another world of motorcycles, of heterosexuality and beer parties, of ambulance rescue that feels so far from my world of emotional facilitation, spiritual endeavors, and living yoga.

I come parallel to Brian's house, my back to it. He is in the yard, adjusting his chainsaw, off to trim trees in storm prep; he shouts above the machine's din. I nod and continue my inching—reach, rake, pull, body more tired now, mid-finger of my right hand complaining.

My various-sized piles of wet leaves dot the middle of the road in a weaving, slipshod fashion, curving and swerving their way forward, mirroring my growing exhaustion. It dawned on me—perhaps Brian doesn't want clumps of leaves in the middle of the road by his house? It always takes some internal effort to reach out to him, some ancient shyness in me activated by his quiet tentativeness. I take a breath and reach inside, pushing my voice above the noise.

"Hey, Brian. Are you okay if I leave the leaves here?"

He shrugs, nods, and continues his adjusting of the saw, which whirs louder, softer, louder again in the midday silence.

I see him consider and, over the saw's noise, he yells something like, ". . . might blow . . . not time . . . get tractor . . ."

Not sure of what he said, I turn back to my task, with that typical post-Brian slight discomfort awakened in me. I never quite know what he means, some part of me pulling away too soon from our interactions, turning from his neutrality and his tentative offerings back to my world of perceived differences.

Reach, rake, pull—faster now, to get down past his house, trying to out-rake my discomfort, not ever sure why there would be discomfort with a guy who has showed up with such helpfulness.

My body gets louder, competing with Brian's saw, lower back tightening, hands crampy. I am lost now in the static of my body's signals and the endless task ahead of me. *Oh, how much more . . . is it over yet*, the child in me wonders.

A cacophony of noise explodes to my left, startling me. To my disbelief, looking over my left shoulder, I see Brian on his riding mower, his mini-tractor, driving in and out of the leaf pilings, blowing them to the right side of the road. Like a passionate cowboy herding cattle, he steers the tractor wildly around and about the leaves, blowing them away from the dreaded ditch.

I am surprised and dumbfounded, as I watch him work. His actions complete my task in an unimagined and powerful way. I am mouth-opened amazed.

He sees me seeing him. His face explodes in a grin from ear to ear. I spontaneously give him a giant thumbs-up. And in that moment, any pieces of me I hold protected and away from him, any perceived differences that have blocked me from him, melt into the afternoon sunlight. We are one, Brian the Tractor Man and Aruni the Rake Woman. Our focus is one: the safety of our neighborhood.

This strange and different man, I think, *a caregiver, our caregiver, a partner in the creation of our neighborhood's safety.*

Team Oak Road, I think.

I turn to shed my tears alone, amazed at the depth of my feeling.

Why am I so amazed? I wonder.

Do I not think I am worth helping?

Do I still hold myself so different and apart from others?

Do I not see our oneness?

The tears continue as I rake myself down the road, realizing that any hope we have for outliving the challenges our country faces rests in this, in community, in the bonding of neighbor with neighbor, no matter our perceived differences, rake and tractor, one, for our common purpose.

The depth of this insight moves me to more tears.

Brian finishes and goes about his day, his red truck kicking up dust on the back road, as I continue down my road.

My feelings subside.

Reach, rake, pull.

Am I almost done, no, not really done, when will I be done?

The questions of a child, I think.

I lean into Oak Road, facing the oncoming storm.

But I do not face it alone.

To be healed we must come with all the other creatures to the feast of Creation.
    —Wendell Berry, *The Art of the Commonplace*

Questions for Your Heart

- Who is your community? Whom do you turn to for unconditional support and love?
- From what kinds of people do you separate yourself?
- How do you separate yourself? Through attitude? Through judgment?
- What would facilitate more connection in your life?

 Practice for Your Life

Give yourself the gift of connecting with one person today. Friend or stranger, allow yourself to locate that place of grace in you and in the other. Practice this. Let the breath support you.

4

The Jews vs. the Yogis vs. the Quakers—Just Kidding

*There is nothing you can ever do or attain that will
get you closer to salvation than it is at this moment.*
—Eckhart Tolle

The silence is softly palpable as it folds all around me, cradling me in its arms. It asks nothing of me, is without demand, expectation or need. It just is—all-including and all-encompassing. Within it there is all the room in the universe for me to find my spot, which turns out to be, remarkably, right where I happen to be sitting.

Someone sneezes. I turn to see one of the members whose large around-the-neck nametag I can't read from this angle, blowing her nose. It is that lovely older woman, gray-haired, who always wears the pantsuits. I don't quite know their names yet, but am more and more able to identify them by their clothing or their characteristic movements. It is an amusing way to get to know people, from inside out, building a platform of silence first upon which words might someday be laid. Or not.

Unlike my temple down the road, in which I am an up-to-date-dues-paying member. There the chatter before services makes me anxious; finding a quick path out at the service's end, skirting circles of talking people, becomes the challenge. The outside air always feels cool, a relief from the stratified air inside the synagogue.

But now—back to the moment. Back to breath. Watch the inhale; exhale. Inhale, exhale. *Or not*, I think with an internal giggle. Eyes open or eyes closed, it does not matter. There is no hierarchy of practice here, no right–wrong. There are simply no techniques here. I come from a yogic tradition of such spiritual techniques. At least, that is how I have imagined it, or needed it to be. Spiritual techniques? Damn, in my work I am a dispenser of spiritual techniques! Yet here, there is nothing to be done, literally.

How many times have I said to people over the years, "There is nothing to do; there is nowhere to go"?

I don't think I knew what that really meant until the first time I sat in this room, this Friends' Meeting Hall in Western Mass., about six months ago.

Like many things in my life, I started going to Meeting because Ras did. My partner does continue to take me to higher levels of experience than those I would willingly access on my own. Sometimes I wonder if I would ever leave the house if Ras weren't continually going places and expecting me to accompany her. And accompany her I do, mostly, except when my resistance wins out and I deem it more important to preserve my precarious status quo and stay home. Although it mostly works in my favor to err on the side of attending something, my habitual response continues to be one of careful self-preservation.

I went to Meeting because she went. And she went because her half-sister, Witchie, had been a Quaker for decades. Good enough reason for both of us. And now I continue to go because it deeply feeds me.

Back to breath, my vehicle of return in meditation. Breathing in, breathing out. So deliciously soft is this moment, so freed of expectation. Thoughts come and go miraculously without much energy to further engage them or without much energy to dissolve them, either:

Wonder what I can get at the Coop for lunch?

Back to breath.

Ras looks cute sitting next to me, so intent.

Back to breath.

I look around, full permission to look. Some people gaze out the windows onto the stunning Berkshire scene—early winter wetland, gray-brown, with rounded hills rising up, sloping, crowning the area. Other folks are looking downward in still contemplation. Still others appear to be sitting with closed eyes, perhaps watching the breath, more the tradition from which I come. Yet the unspoken permission to do it, to simply sit in contemplation in any way, frees me up to relax without judgment into this, my moment.

I think of meditating in my community in the days of the ashram. I can feel the anxiety, sitting among the people I loved so much, the people whose approval I needed so deeply. There was a right–wrong alive in me in those days; a paradigm that my aging just refuses to sustain today. Just remembering it brings a tightness to my belly, some sweat to my palms. I was so sure I was a yogic fraud, that no meditation was going on inside me, only frantic attempts to be quiet, to suppress the cough exploding in my throat, to do it right, and ultimately and most importantly, to be accepted. It was an exhausting struggle, one that I always seemed to lose, trying to hide my self-defined deficiencies from my community.

But not here. Here without apparent doctrine, here without rules or without dues statements or requests for money like my temple, here I can just sit.

This thought brings a wave of emotion over me. I feel strangely touched, almost weepy.

Someone stands up; I shift my attention.

Matthew. Middle-aged, pot-bellied, a man with the bluest-of-robin's-egg-blue eyes—the eyes of a meditator, I instantly thought, upon meeting him. Eyes that obviously see with clarity, deeply, both inside and out. And a man who wears strangely fluorescent clothing, of all sorts. Today over his khaki pants he wears a smock-like shirt, cut in a plunging scoop neck with blossoming sleeves, in a fascinating shade of fuchsia. Under it he wears your fundamental New-England–like turtleneck one might find in an *L.L. Bean* catalogue, in your basic shade of ivory.

After standing for a few moments, his words softly slice the silence open:

"Light opens the dark. Light permeates the dark. And the dark becomes the light . . ."

He continues for a few more sentences. I am unable to follow the words, because my heart has so fully leapt up to embrace him. I am deeply moved not so much by the literal meaning of his contribution but by the depth from which his words emerge. His essence seems to have engaged mine.

I allow the tears. Tears . . . of what? Of connection? Or unity? How could it be that I feel more connected, more received, more *simpatico* here than with my Jewish community at the temple hardly a block down the road?

I think of my temple. I am a Jew, I know, from inside, out. The eyes from which I see the world are Jewish eyes. The humor with which I meet it, the sensibility with which I move through it—all are Jewish. I live as a Jew on this planet. This I know. And this I love. Sitting in synagogue, oh, how my body knows the Jewish melodies, rejoicing with them. My heart knows the Hebrew chants, much more deeply than my head. A core of me relaxes, almost thaws, when I attend services. Yet I sit separate in that congregation. I sit and I thaw alone. Or so it seems.

I weep a bit more. *Perhaps these are tears of grieving,* I consider. *Grieving for the community of Jews that never was meant for me.*

Maybe because I'm a lesbian, I consider, trying to understand this split.

Or if I joined a committee. The Jewish response to challenges in life.

The *what if's* trail off into silence. I let them be. The thoughts shift and change.

We continue to sit. I am awash in the swirls of thought regarding the truth of my tri-affiliation: I am a Jew, a Yogi, and an Almost-Friend.

The meeting ends with a lovely ritual. When the hour is reached, the clerk stands, and walks toward another, extending his hand and offering, "Good morning, friend." All participants turn toward each other with extended hand and heart. It is a powerful and touching process for me weekly.

This week I extend my hand and heart toward Liz on my left, a stunningly smiling young black woman, and Shirley, an octogenarian in front of me. Making eye contact with others around me, I savor this ritual.

I unsuccessfully hide my tears.

Weeks pass. Chanukah arrives, bringing with it the spirit of returning light. Ras and I light candles in my mother's menorah, my childhood candleholder, night after night. We lustily sing the blessing while making up our own fluid translation, happily revising it nightly. We do this beneath the shadow of our tiny Christmas tree, sheltered and safe from canine intervention, snacking or nibbling, on the elevated island in our kitchen.

The next weekend, we attend the Friends' Holiday Party. Not surprisingly, I find myself slightly resistant, wanting to stay home rather than interact with people without the structure of a meeting. Nevertheless I walk in the door with Ras, bringing our offering of deviled eggs, slightly seasonally askew, yet our primary and most effective contribution to potlucks. Sitting in the big meditation room, now filled with Christmas caroling, I breathe and try to relax, almost wishing I were home.

I'm good with Christmas, I think. *I'm making up for lost time from the deprivation of my Jewish childhood, my separation from the dominant culture's holiday blast.*

Finding out almost innocently these past weeks that Jesus is a part of the Friend's doctrine has upset me. *Jesus is fine, but not for me,* I think. *Too contradictory to my upbringing.*

In this room of connection, I feel separate tonight. I take a breath and launch into the next carol.

"Oh, come all ye faithful—joyful and triumphant—come ye oh come ye to Bethlehem."

I'm acting as if. It's okay, it's just a little sad.

"Oh, I see you are celebrating two holidays tonight," says a voice off to my right.

I turn to look. The wife of one of the pillars of the meeting, Elaine, introduces herself to me, as she points toward my Chanukah socks, adorned with Jewish stars and menorahs in lovely sequence. I laugh.

"I'm going to have the ham here, than scoot over to my temple's Chanukah celebration for potato latkes," she offers, leaning closer.

We laugh together, so grateful I am for her kind reaching out.

I realize in this moment that there is no deprivation here in my life. This moment of my growth is one of inclusivity. I am old enough now to give myself full permission to integrate it all. To savor, to pick and choose, to put it all together. Not without feelings, not without disappointment and grieving, not without hope and possibility—yet it is all sacred. It is all inevitable. All these streams of influence, all these rivers of practices and feelings and perspectives. I get them all.

I think of the word *versus*. In its Latin root, *ventere*, its past participle means *to turn, to change*, rather than the oppositional meaning we hold today.

I get to turn; I get to change. I get to continue to choose what touches me and what grows me, continually building on the platform of who I am.

"Ah," I hear myself saying to Elaine. "Ah, yes. We get it all, don't we?"

We get it all.

Yes, we get it all.

———————————

There is no other happiness here in this moment
Than to be free of the thought
That I am different from you.

—Ulpaladeva's Shiva-Stotra

Questions for Your Heart

- What streams of influence have affected your personal life? Your professional life? Your spiritual practice?
- Can you see how one stream of influence has merged into another?
- What does the line, "We get it all," mean in your world?
- Are there arenas in your life where you don't "get it all"? How does that happen? Of what do you deprive yourself?

 Practice for Your Life

Consider: are there any new ideas or beliefs coming into your personal, professional, or spiritual worlds? How might you encourage new currents of possible perspectives?

5

Work—It's All True

Be kind, for everyone you meet is fighting a hard battle.
—Anonymous

The voice on the other end of the phone crackles, fades in and out, and reestablishes itself again.

Ah, the curse of my client's Bluetooth, I think. I can grab every third word and build the sentence from my felt-sense of her narrative. I pick and choose words, creating sentences from her ramblings.

"And then . . . finished the . . . didn't feel . . . but I knew . . ." she continues, laying down her breadcrumb clues. Like Hansel-and-Gretel-Merged, I wearily follow them, working my way out of the woods of this coaching session, toward this hour's blessed completion.

Any technological attempts I have made to render our literal phone connection more functional have failed. Asking her to repeat herself grows old quickly during a fifty-minute session, too.

Which comes first, emotional disconnection or a faulty cell phone reception, I wonder? *The chicken or the egg?*

"So then I will . . ." she offers.

I jump in with some feeble attempt at support. It's not difficult for me to support people; that is not the challenge for me in my coaching practice. The challenge is to be there for all people. Actually the real challenge is being there for all people, all the time. Saying this aloud strips it down to its natural absurdity—how could one do that? How could one be there for all people, all of the time? Yet that is what I expect of myself.

Some people are really easy to connect with. Some are not. Isn't this completely obvious? Is this obvious to everyone but not to me?

Am I justifying? Am I out of integrity? Am I in it for the money, not willing to turn away a paying client?

I am not always 100 percent sure. Living with the contradictions that life offers me—and living with the contradictions that work shows me—is a challenging practice.

Work offers us such inconsistencies. There is nothing to do but to bear them, to do our best, and to go home at the end of the day.

Let me simply say that I am ambivalent. On the subject of my work, I think and feel things that may contradict each other—that may even contradict themselves. I find it very challenging to have mixed responses and mixed feelings about the circumstances in my life. But the older I get, the more I realize ambivalence is inevitable and rich with opportunities for emotional insight and growth.

The bottom line is simply that sometimes my coaching sessions work really well, and sometimes they work well enough.

I find myself uncomfortable talking about this. There is a part of me that thinks I need to be beyond-clear and beyond-super-functional 2000 percent of the time. Anything short of this would be lack of clarity (God forbid!) or slacking off. I am truly a tough one to live with. *Well enough* is not a comfortable zone for me to inhabit. Seeing these, my character challenges, through the mirror of my coaching practice, is powerfully and insightfully uncomfortable.

But what is work but a shiny mirror, in which we can see ourselves, our patterns, our flaws, and our strengths? What is work but the daily onslaught/insight into ways to be more completely who we really are?

In the mirror of my coaching work, I clearly see the impossible standards I set for myself. I would never expect from another person such levels of consistent perfection. Perhaps it's because things come easily to me. This is not to say that I do not struggle. I do struggle like crazy, yet, when it's time to dive into a project, be it teaching, writing, or coaching, I find that Zone of Presence fairly effortlessly and fairly comfortably. Perhaps, because things are essentially easy for me, my ancient urge to do more, to do "better" is incrementally increased.

I exhaust myself.

And then, the hardest of all things to talk about, not just about the ways I feel I am an out-of-integrity, internal slacker, but the times in which, by my simply being a presence, my client zooms through to the next level of growth and development. How can I possibly talk about these situations, which happen consistently, without a "gosh-golly-it-wasn't-really-me" kind of false humility? My tendency is to never speak of these things!

Here's Donna in a coaching session, her dearest husband, Jim, diagnosed with lung cancer a few months before:

It was terrifying . . . waiting with him during his first chemo session. He was so quiet, didn't say a word . . . he's usually so talkative, can't shut up! I just sat there and held his hand, like you and I talked about the last week. It was so helpful to have had some time with you beforehand to think about being there with more intention. I sat with him; I did pray, like you suggested. The 23rd Psalm really helped me, even though I could hardly spit it out . . . at least I had something to do with my mind. Jim eventually fell asleep. I continued to try to breathe—thanks for that email reminder this morning—and continued the prayer. We got through the session. We'll get through this, I guess. I'm so grateful to have your support . . .

Offering Donna an anchor to ground her in her terror, some strategies about how to manage her accelerating cycle of stress, and some practical responses to the completely shifted geographical logistics of her life is effortless for me. I know my presence and support continues to help move her forward through this devastating and challenging time in her life.

There are some things we just can't do alone; some situations life gives us are just too untenable to navigate solo. And we don't necessarily know that, we willful, strong-minded, all-powerful-and-all-potent Western people.

So can I rest with this? Can I take in the fact that I am helpful, effective, and successful in my coaching relationship with Donna? I can—with some edgy discomfort.

Here's another coaching example: Susan. At age thirty-five, Susan has been hugely successful in the cutthroat world of corporate finance. She came to our coaching relationship-driven, exhausted, and overwhelmed, unable to be available to the kindness offered to her by her mild-mannered husband and unable to prioritize her personal life at all. Simply said, work owned her life. Work had won. Susan, unaware of these underlying issues, created her coaching goals around work, what a surprise—to create strategies to manage her quick-to-anger boss, and to manage her staff with less stress and bother.

For a few sessions, we focused together on these more superficial yet nevertheless pressing issues of her boss and her need for exercise. I felt as if we were going through the motions of someone else's script, but it was where Susan was. Mindfulness meets us where we are—there was nothing to do but to continue unraveling her process with her. We drafted some responses she could offer her boss without thinking, some ways she could create more boundaries with him, and some consistent and more intentional ways she could regularly meet with staff.

Somewhere in our second or third month together, as this first layer of discomfort quieted down, her denial around her compulsive overwork patterns began to crack. Here is Susan:

> *I don't know what's happening . . . I woke in the middle of the night—I looked at Jeff next to me in bed—it was as if I didn't know him or couldn't remember my life with him—I went to the bathroom and sobbed for an hour—I don't know why—I was able to hold some good boundaries at work today—got to the gym, too—but I'm feeling so empty—so lonely—so haunted. I have everything I ever wanted—how could I feel so bad— what's going on here?*

Susan was now open to a mindful, non-judgmental appraisal of her work/life balance. We proceeded quietly through this phase of her coaching. I had absolutely no agenda and no perceived outcome for her. I just walked the path with her.

Eleven months after Susan began coaching, life finds her in a very different place. She has limited the scope of her job, finally willing to be responsible for less and to be satisfied with a reduced salary. This, along with her growing capacity to delegate, has lessened her job-centered stress a good deal. She is having more fun with Jeff and is much more willing to relax at home.

Surprisingly, Susan has made the commitment to work with her compulsivity with food. This was an issue that I wasn't even aware of. She is getting support from a nutritionist and some mindfulness groups. It's a good thing I was not in charge of this agenda or its outcome—this one I would have completely overlooked!

Susan is in a process of rebalancing and of attending to her real needs. It's a miracle; my presence supported this process to unfold.

Work, employment, labor, job, vocation, occupation—be you freelancing or fully plugged in, be you self-employed or one of many in a large organization—if you work primarily with your hands or with your brain—if you work indoors or out—if you are working to feed your stomach or to feed your soul, or both; no matter what it is that you do, work is the water in which you daily swim in the currents of life. Give yourself a break; recognize how well you are doing by just showing up.

Blow bubbles. Relax and play.

Aim for the other shore and breathe.

Give yourself full permission to show up and do your best.

Live with the contradictions that work shows you.

Bear the inconsistencies that life offers you.

Like whom you like—it doesn't have to be everyone.

Do your best—you don't have to be perfect.

All these shades of presence that are revealed at work—they are all inevitable.

They are all sacred.

They are all true.

See how much you can relax with each of your work moments, no matter what it might bring you.

———————

Happiness is when what you think, what you say, and what you do are in harmony.

—Mahatma Gandhi

Questions for Your Heart

- What is a recent victory you have had at work?
- What is a current challenge you face in this arena?
- How are you critical of yourself at work? Is it hard to acknowledge your professional successes?
- What is a hope or a prayer that you have for yourself in the workplace?

 Practice for Your Life

Take a current challenge at work, a difficult person or thing, and look for the mirror in it. What is the lesson that it is reflecting back to you?

Practice reframing *challenge* to *lesson*.

6

More to Learn

We claim spiritual progress not spiritual perfection.
—The Big Book of Alcoholics Anonymous

"Really? Come on. After all these years? What's up with you?"

I kick the clump of snow with my boot. Standing outside my car, I want to magically whisk myself into its insides, and be snatched away from this one-sided conversation.

"Well, why? Why do you still go? Are you hiding out there? Aren't there other places to put your attention or energy or time?"

There are not many people in my life who confront me on this issue. My sister just goes silent on the topic. But Mary Ellen, a friend from work, occasionally pushes this edge with me. For some reason, with her, I get quiet, wanting to protect rather than explain my choice.

"Hey, I gotta get headed home. Gotta walk the dogs before it gets too dark," I finally say, snapped out of my silence, reaching for the icy door handle. "Really, I have to go."

She eyes me coolly, as I reach into the car for my windshield scraper. The day has dumped a thin layer of gritty ice onto my car.

Not a problem for driving, I think. *It just keeps me in this conversation longer.*

Mary Ellen is not leaving. Finally I turn and face her. The words come on my breath:

"I go because I grow there. I go because it is my choice to go there. I go because it is my gift to go there," I offer her, as I turn back to the car now, investing elbow grease and wildly scraping away at the ice-grit on the windshield.

After a few beats of her silence, I look over my shoulder to measure her response. Her eyebrow lifts to meet the red plaid cap she has pulled low over her head. It's a funny image to me—eyebrow and the redness of cap, one line. I snicker.

"Oh, funny, right," she says, missing the source of my laughter. But we laugh together now, somehow amused by ourselves.

She lightens up, waves, and continues trekking up the hill, to the farthest parking lot way above.

"See ya tomorrow," I call after her, as I continue scratching away at the car. *She's a good soul,* I think.

And it is a good question to consider:

Why *do* I keep going?

I smile again.

Why wouldn't I?

The price for this lifetime of grace I have been given, it seems, is simply attendance at my Twelve Step meetings. Obviously it's not a literal price. Nobody collects my ticket at the door and crosses me off some cosmic, energetic list somewhere. Yet for me, simply by driving toward a meeting, I begin to feel realigned and reconnected to deeper knowing, to a deeper access of a positive perspective and a faith that works.

I got sober a long time ago. Twelve Step program saved me from a life of choice-less addiction. Little did I know when I walked into that room that I would be given so much more than just a life free from the pain of alcohol and drug addiction. So much more! It saved me and it continues to save me from a life of horrible decisions, ruined relationships, zero self-esteem, and doomed career hopes. Little did I know that I would be given a fluid and alive plan for living, for being in right relationship with reality, for leading a spiritual life grounded in caring, useful relationships.

Little did I know.

I just wanted the pain to stop. The pain did stop. And then the real work began. And so it continues.

My relationship to Twelve Step program is the only place in my life in which I am fully and totally non-conflicted. I have absolutely no ambivalence whatsoever about the nature of the Program and its relationship to my life—my life in the past, in the present, and in the future. I am absolutely positive that I get exactly what I need there to have an extraordinary and wondrous life. I believe that, as I keep attending meetings, I will be given the skills to get through the greatest challenge I face, the many nameless dimensions of aging that the upcoming years will bring me. It's pretty fabulous to have a place of such clarity. Yet again, I am blessed by my addiction—without that, none of these tools, gifts, and possibilities would emerge.

Of course, I go through dry spells, challenging times, when I feel disconnected from myself, from the Program, from others, from life, and from Grace. But as I keep going through the flow of my practices—meditation, talking to other recovering people, and attending meetings—it changes. The arid spell opens up; an oasis emerges, as I outlive my own disconnection.

My tendency is to not talk about my relationship to Program. It isn't because of our tradition of anonymity as much as it is some self-consciousness that arises for me. It all sounds too—simplistic? Too Pollyanna-ish? Too cultish? Too gloating?

I don't know. I just know that by keeping Twelve Steps as the foundation of my life, every single challenge I have been given has opened up into an eventual blessing, waiting to happen. I have been given the skills and the tools to get through my very real and lengthening life.

The literature in the Program doesn't specifically talk about long-term sobriety and ongoing attendance. The invitation is simple: keep coming. I don't know the percentage of people who achieve long-term sober time and stop regularly attending meetings. I actually believe I could probably not drink, if I were to stop going to meetings today. But why would I risk it? Why would I compromise the quality of my life? Why would I deprive myself of such a rich ocean of support, wisdom, and community? And why would I choose to make life so much harder than it has to be? It is also my responsibility to give back to others that which I have been so freely given. By attending meetings, I am there for others, as they and others have been there for me. That cycle, that circle of healing brings a profoundly rich vein of meaning to my life.

I'm sitting at the Thursday night meeting. We're in a drafty meeting room of an old church. Billy is a gravelly voiced man, short and compact in body, lined face tanned by years of outdoor work.

We have a few minutes before the meeting begins and we are talking about long term sobriety. He has several decades of sober time, and continues to faithfully and happily attend meetings. He's telling one of his famous-Billy-stories. I lean in closer to catch each word:

> *When I was newly sober in Boston, I would see these guys with years and years of (sober) time. I didn't get it at all. Why would they still keep comin'? Don't you ever graduate from this place? I remember lookin' at them and wonderin' about them—gettin' so much from them, too, at the same time, from their stories. Their laughter! How it pissed me off that they laughed so much! Didn't they know how miserable I was? But somethin' about their laughter gave me hope. Or somethin'.*

I readjust my weight on the wooden church chair. Billy is a compelling storyteller. I am riveted, caught by his every word.

> *And there was this one guy, Franny was his name. An old-timer. I remember him so well. He was so upbeat, so positive. I couldn't believe anyone could be that positive about life. I was eyein' him for a while after meetings, tryin' to get up enough nerve to talk with him. Finally one night after our men's group, I did.*
>
> *"Franny, hey, I want to ask you somethin'."*
>
> *He was all ears.*
>
> *"How come you guys keep comin'? How come you keep goin' to meetings?"*
>
> *The guy's face lit up—there was some spark in his blue eyes that just seemed to get brighter and brighter.*
>
> *He leaned toward me and said in his Boston accent, "More to learn, son. There just keeps being more to learn."*

Billy and I crack up at the folk brilliance of this simple yet profound message. The meeting is getting ready to start. I bid my farewell to Billy and face the chairperson, touched by another piece of Twelve Step lore.

The meeting carries me.

Winter slowly unfolds.

I find myself in an ongoing funk, one which, like slimy quicksand, wants me at the bottom of its mire. I poke my nose above the mess, gasp at some air, and am pulled down again. This life moment, the opportunity to grow, has all the elements of profoundly painful trigger for me: salary, salary inequity, and confusing messages from the upper administration of my place of employment. I go to meetings—talk to people. I find ways to release my expectations, feel released from the negative internal dialogue and relax for a few days. Then another administrative miscommunication sends me spinning. The negative, old tapes increase in volume inside my head:

Don't you see how hard I work? Don't you realize who I am? Don't you see the value of my contribution? Change this. This can't happen. Change it. Now.

There is nothing wrong with those habitual responses, but they are not forward-moving. They do not put me in the place in which I choose to live. They don't put me in the solution of this issue, which is to put out my truth, to communicate it clearly, and to let go of the results. I need to practice one of my core beliefs: that life is here to bless me. Even the most difficult of circumstances offers a doorway to growth and possibility. Yet when money is in the mix, this practice gets much more challenging for me.

I'm bummed out. I've lost my surrender! I'm reengaged in this internal warfare, mumbling and grumbling at life. This is not a place in which I choose to live. But I am here now, this gray Saturday morning, as I drive toward my home group meeting, a meeting I have consistently attended for many years now. The Berkshire land, always a balm to my spirit, unfolds unnoticed around me as I drive. Several executives from work seem to be alive in my mind—I am having clear and meaningful exchanges with them. But they are not here. They are elsewhere, probably having a fine moment. I am not. I am not living in reality.

I navigate the church parking lot dotted with mounds of dirty snow, get out of the car, and sludge into the meeting. I find my seat, instantly annoyed by Anita, sitting next to me, who turns toward me and brightly says, "I'm so excited by 2013!"

Yuck, says my internal grumbler. *Don't you see I am miserable right now? Spare me your positivity.*

The meeting opens. This is probably my favorite place to be in the universe. Yes, in the universe, a universe that includes Cinnamon Bay in St. John or Flamingo Bay in Puerto Rico, its white beach extending, curving, hugging the blue-green water. I love this room, a big old church hall, with its huge picture of Jesus behind us, literally guarding our backs. But today, for now, I keep my emotional distance. Arms crossed over my chest, an invisible warning to all, I sit contained and committed to my struggle. We sit in a ragtag circle, about thirty of us. The reading is about the power of attitude. *Great, frigging attitude*, I think. I manage to block myself from the words of the first few people who share. Nothing is penetrating. A part of me is committed to that, to holding on to my distance and separation, to my fury at reality for not granting me a giant and public pay hike.

Then Charlie shares. His already short crew cut is buzzed down to his scalp, but for a little Dennis-the-Menace clump at the top of his head. I respect him—he is a deep and good man, with a clear way of expressing himself. But I am committed to my separateness here, wrapped in my own self-imposed struggle.

Charlie talks about something unfolding in his work, some old project come back for re-inspection and re-evaluation. He was freaking out, trying really hard to figure out how to manipulate the situation so he wouldn't be in the limelight. He had a few really rough days, trying to figure out how to fib his way out of this issue. And then, as he describes, the situation shifted:

> *I talked to a few people. They all reminded me that I didn't have to control this, that I couldn't change it. They reminded me, each in their own way, that whatever happened as the outcome of this evaluation would be all right. One of them said to me—"Charlie, you get to decide how you go through this. This is your decision. Struggle if you like. But you don't have to. Make a choice about how you want to go through this process. And do it."*

> *And when he said that to me,* Charlie says, his blue flannel shirt cascading around him, *the most extraordinary thing happened. Everything changed. Everything changed drastically. In that moment. Like, reality itself changed.*

> *It reminded me of a time, years ago, when I was hiking in the desert in Arizona. We went into a cave. I turned my headlight on, and yet the light was so weak. I could hardly see. I was really confused. Why was my new headlight not shining a brighter light into this cave? Then I realized I had my sunglasses on. As soon as I took them off, everything changed! The shift was*

profound and dramatic. Reality changed. And that was exactly what happened the other day, when I decided that I didn't have to fight this situation. I would do my best. I would communicate clearly. And I would let go of the outcome.

Tears flood my eyes. Charlie, this perfect stranger, has offered me exactly the piece of emotional and energetic data that I need to shift the moment, to choose a more spacious and comfortable and enjoyable moment. I feel the separation melt around me. I feel bathed in the warmth of this Fellowship of Grace, surrounded by folks without last names, who give me, on a daily basis, exactly what I need to live a life second to none. To live my life.

I blow my nose, settle into my seat, nod to Anita, and listen with new ears.

I decide to take off my sunglasses.

––––––––––––––

Surely goodness and mercy shall follow you all the days of your life; and you shall dwell in the House of Grace forever.
                                                     —The 23rd Psalm

Questions for Your Heart

- What is the biggest arena of struggle in your life? Consider it through the lens of non-judgmental awareness.
- What supports you in realigning with how you want to live, in releasing the struggle? Is it books? Music? Friends? A spiritual connection or teaching? An attitude reframe?
- Is there one small step you can take today to begin reframing your attitude about this struggle?
- Can you remember a time in which you mindfully shifted your attitude to a more positive one? How did this work? How did it feel?

 Practice for Your Life

Bring your attention to a struggle in your life. What would a positive attitude look like for you? Practice doing this today. What do you observe? What might you learn?

7

Rail Against the Man/Not

You are perfect just as you are and you can use a little improvement.
—Shunryu Suzuki Roshi

I can feel the heat building under my hairline. My jaw tightens. The sound of my back teeth grinding on themselves gets louder inside my head. A little trickle of sweat slips and slides down my spine.

A loud, internal "Grrrrrrrrrrrrrrrrrr" grows in my belly.

This is not good, every cell in my body is screeching.

I look to my left. The flushed face of Molly, the head of the Human Resources department turns toward me. With a forced half-grin and a nod of attempted shared conspiracy she meets my eyes. Not willing to engage, I look away, more aware of physical reactions inside my body than the external words of Mark.

Mark! The new COO seems to pontificate. His index finger gestures in the air, his pointed chin appearing to make exclamation marks after each passionate sentence he utters.

Knowing it's not true, I nevertheless want to make this whole messy experience about—him.

I wiggle against the tan corduroy couch, attempting to awaken my own awareness. *Wake up*, I demand of myself, inhaling a strong breath.

"Changes in the department . . . *blah* . . . *blah* . . . *blah* . . . not meeting the bottom line . . . need for belt-tightening . . . *blah* . . . *blah* . . . *blah*." So speaks Mark. I hear every fourth word through newly cotton-ized ears.

I am not happy, I think. I have an internal snicker, thinking of Mia, my grand-niece. At age three-and-a-half, when her baby brother came home from the hospital, she stamped around the house repeatedly reporting, "I am not happy."

I am three-and-a-half years old right now.

I attempt some feeble rebuttal, stammer and stutter some comments, knowing the words, as I hear them leave my mouth, are disconnected from my power and from my truth. I am literally struck speechless, quite a surprising state for the usually loquacious me.

After all these years of deep and committed service to this organization, why would I receive so big a salary cut?

At my age? Really?

Don't they know who I am?

My internal response is fueled with righteous indignation, quite different from my external one, my words sounding to my own ears as almost submissive. Or, to be kinder to myself, perhaps I am simply inappropriately unresponsive.

The meeting has ended, I am told. I find my way to the door, flushed and befuddled.

The cooler temperature in the hallway shocks me awake. *Why am I embarrassed?* I ask myself, angry not at them, but at myself.

They should be embarrassed, not me, I think.

But, despite my intellectual understanding of the moment, my face is flaming with a senseless shame.

The day unfolds with mumbled confusion. When explaining the situation to several trustworthy friends, I seem to have huge gaps in understanding. It doesn't make sense. Wasn't I listening? Didn't I take it in? The pieces don't add up. Did I miss something?

I feel foolish and useless, unable to advocate for myself.

The roller coaster of feelings, ever changing, always morphing, overtakes me. I spend an almost-sleepless night furious, tossing, turning, mumbling and cursing the Others, the Ones Who Have Done This To Me. I am righteous and clear at 2:00 AM, indignant at 3:00, brilliant and charismatic at 4:00. At 7:00 AM, dressed and rumpled, I am exhausted and defeated by my own hyper-vigilant mind. Thinking the worst about myself and the world around me has not been a successful life strategy. Yet it has been a first and obviously essential reaction to this trauma.

This next day finds me humbled, collapsed beneath the weight of it. Life is heavy; I pull myself around the hallways at work, show-ing up just minimally for my responsibilities—one Share Circle to facilitate, a meeting, one coaching client. I find myself slightly and reluctantly engaged with life around me.

I am defeated.

Somewhere during the second night, sleeping finally, I awaken to the voice of Grace: *It will be fine. It always will be fine. As you let go, more will be given to you. Trust this.*

I know the truth of this. I live on a platform of years' worth of evidence of its truth. Clearly I have not been carried this far on my journey of mindful self-discovery to be dropped on my head and left penniless in retirement. Surely it will work out. I close my eyes, practicing my breath—inhale/one, two, three, four/exhale, one, two, three, four.

But I am sick of my breath.

The next day I awake drained. *Beaten into submission*, I think. Yet it is an easier day, one that flows with fewer bumps and grinds and twists of feelings. Sleep helps, of course, I notice. My teaching is more fun, my coaching clients more interesting.

I guess this is surrender, I think. *Let it be*, the Beatles said. *They were right. Right?*

I don't know. But it feels better to not rail against reality.

I get an email from my new boss, Mary, who has been beyond-eager to advocate for me yet without enough leveraged authority to seemingly impact the situation. She asks if I can attend a 10:00 meeting of the Senior Leadership Council in her place, since she is locked into responding to a family emergency.

"Yes," I unwillingly respond, emailing wildly. "I can attend half of it, since I'm teaching at 11:00."

Damn.

My history with this organization is complex. Having once been part of executive administration, released from that upper echelon seven years ago by the then-incoming CEO through a painful and public downsizing of role and salary, I have for these past years served in a direct guest contact role. It has been a glorious freedom to live in the essence of the organization's mission. I am almost always fully relieved to be released from the leadership of this organization—except when I'm not, except when envy sneaks into me. This envy is usually based in salary comparison, which is a guaranteed not-pretty road for me to travel.

It is time for the meeting. I walk into the Conference Room. It is packed with eighteen people, with space and air enough for not quite three-quarters of that number. We sit catawampusly staggered in our folding chairs, squashed along the double length of conference tables. I look around at these folks, the "Cultural and Functional Leaders" of the organization, as our CEO introduces them. Most of them have been here a few years, unlike my two-and-a-half decades. The woman I sit next to is unknown to me—I have never seen her before.

I say to her, "Who are you?", missing perhaps any tone of rudeness this comment might carry. Newly hired, she says, directing the creative brand of the organization. I imagine her salary is three times mine.

There's that completely not pretty road of salary comparison, I think. *Don't go there.*

I ride the waves of the first hour of this meeting. I attempt to take basic notes of the proceedings, a budget and department summary, for my boss. This task keeps me grounded and slightly focused. My feelings run the gamut, from envy to annoyance, to justified self-righteousness, to some eventual quieting of my mind. I realize, with profound relief, that I don't have to stay here. At 10:50, I am freed.

I watch the clock creep toward my liberation. It sneaks, it crawls, it tiptoes its way toward my emancipation. I practice leaving in my mind. I see myself getting up and turning away from the density, the complexity of the running of a complicated, multi-income-stream organization. I am growing more and more excited with each passing moment.

10:50 does arrive, smack in the middle of the new vice president of development's (four times my salary) presentation. I stand and turn, giddily relieved, and make my way, in two movements, toward the door. In one motion, I am out in the cool hall, celebrating my liberation.

I dash happily toward the Forest Room, to facilitate the Share Circle. This is a mindful communication activity, in which the guests are guided to look inside, to report out their experience of the moment, without response to each other. It is probably one of my favorite things to lead, one of the most satisfying parts of my job.

There are several guests waiting for me in the already-set-up circle of chairs. I greet them heartedly, truly delighted to be with them. Waiting to begin, I am in awe of the disparity between the Conference Room and the Forest Room, between the Senior Leadership Council and this seemingly random group of guests. Here there is air, breath of connection, permission to feel. In the Conference Room, strategies are being created, budgets analyzed, departments dismantled and reassembled.

Obviously you can't have one without the other—the administration creates the structure, the business in which this experience and many more unfold. I understand that. Yet I am profoundly touched by where I have been placed. Life has deposited me here in the heart, in the essence of the mission.

I feel tears rush into my eyes.

By the time we begin, we are fifteen people, fourteen plus me, strangers on the path, brought together for this fifty-minute individual and collective dive into shared mindfulness.

With each passing moment I feel more relaxed into the available grace of this group.

I focus on the guests, on the circle.

I do the things I do so well and so effortlessly: I greet, I welcome, I introduce, I explain, I lead, I model, I relax. I allow the process to unfold, and unfold, it does.

The first woman begins to share:

"Sometimes I feel like such a victim in my life. I almost can't catch my breath," says Kathy, a pale thirty-something young woman from Chicago. "Things that happen at my work with my wacky boss—things with my boyfriend. It's as if I have no voice. But it's changing." She smiles slightly, shyly. "No—*I* am changing. I am learning to speak my truth, to say aloud my perspective. Everything changes when I change."

Nods happen all around as her witnesses hold her in accepting silence. To be felt, to be heard and seen, to be received is a potent and healing balm for one's heart.

Jim, his face creased, silver hair in a buzz cut, speaks next. He is an older man from Long Island and he says:

"Ever since my wife died, my life is so different."

The group takes an almost collective sigh of support for this perfect stranger.

"She did so much. She managed our calendar, she got us out with friends. It's such an adjustment without her. But I am finding my way—doing okay. I'm beginning to realize what I need, what I want. I'm lonely, of course. But I'm . . ." He hesitates, tears building.

"But I'm beginning to speak aloud what I need. I never had to do that before. She did it for me."

When Jim finishes, we take a collective breath with him. Bridges are built from heart to heart, from younger to older, from Chicago to Long Island, all around the circle. By speaking the truth, doorways to connection open.

The sharing continues, heart-felt and authentic. I feel warm and relaxed and deeply touched.

I am deeply awakened by Kathy and by Jim's sharing. My truth sneaks into me, revealing itself from inside, out: in this moment I know what I need to do next in response to this intended salary cut: I need to speak my truth. It never dawned on me until this moment that this was an option.

I have to speak my truth!

Just as Kathy and Jim reminded me, I have to say aloud my perspective, my understanding of my worth in this organization. I have to contest it.

This is my work, I think. *This is my value. Facilitating, teaching, coaching—not the big bucks, I realize—but essential to the core of this establishment.*

I am at the core of this establishment. That has value.

That has profound worth.

I feel myself sitting up straighter. My next steps emerge. Write a letter. Speak my truth. Ask for a review. And if I need the support, I could even get a lawyer, a crazy option, but an option nevertheless. And then, after I take more right action, I will be able to surrender more authentically to the outcome.

The never-ending saga of my emerging truth cracks me up.

I have a little chuckle, settle more deeply into my chair, and continue doing what I do best.

I continue loving these guests.

––––––––––––

Bless you; change me.
—Twelve Step wisdom, to be used in a moment of irritation

Questions for Your Heart

- What do you rail against? Where do you fight reality and want life to be different?
- Are there places in your life where you withhold from speaking your truth?
- Is there one particular person with whom you tend to be less than authentic?
- What words might you speak to this person to become more real?

 ## Practice for Your Life

Close your eyes, breathe, and relax. Imagine you can snuggle into this moment. With every breath, wrap yourself more deeply in a blanket of radical self-compassion. From this place of Self, enter this doorway on the power of your breath.

In order to more comfortably relax into reality, is there a prayer, an intention, or a hope that you hold for yourself in this moment? If so, offer that prayer onto the altar of your own heart.

8

100 Years Later—Sort Of

Barn's burned. Now I can see the moon.
—Mizuta Masahide

In a retro and deeply déjà vu–like kind of way, it is all tremendously exciting. I attempt to keep myself in check, to not appear too frivolously engaged. I don't know why. I guess I am simply attempting to carefully monitor my emotional reaction to this odd day's proceedings.

Wearing white to acknowledge the spirituality and sanctity of the guru—it's been a while!—I feel uncomfortable and strangely self-conscious. My yoga pants tighten around my thighs as I walk, mimicking my building hesitation. My white fleece top, respecting the frigid January temperatures, feels wrong, out of place, too thickly functional and not daintily respectful enough.

Seventeen years ago.

One hundred years ago.

Two landmark dates frame this day.

Seventeen years ago the man who was our guru, our living spiritual teacher, was ousted by the Board of Directors of this organization, due to his misuse of power. It was not pretty. Hearts were broken; lives were ruined. Promises, deeply given, were shattered beneath the weight of his misuse of sexuality, greed, and manipulation. For the first time in my then-forty-eight years, I began to understand the meaning of trauma, as it coldly seeped into my bones. It was described to us in those days and weeks after the upheaval as, "an event that happens after which all is changed." Clearly everything as I understood it was now changed in my post-guru world. Well, almost everything. As a member of Twelve Step program, my platform of recovery was strongly in place. That commitment only deepened, as the ground I walked upon in the ashram shimmered and shook with seismographic tremors.

And one hundred years ago, the man who was this guru's teacher, the Guy Who Was the Real Deal, was born. Swami Kripalu would be one hundred years old today. He was an Indian guru of prominence and renown, with thousands of disciples in India practicing his teachings of *Sanatan Dharma*, the honoring of the whole world as one family. The former ashram, now the yoga and health center at which I work, is hosting a celebration weekend, culminating in this Sunday afternoon celebration. Former residents of the ashram have been invited back to honor and appreciate this good man's profound teachings and remarkable service to the world. This is noteworthy, since it is the first time in these seventeen years that attention is formally being given to our spiritual roots and the community that formed it.

I am ambivalent. I wouldn't miss this day for the world and have been greatly awaiting it. Yet I feel shy and remarkably awkward as I enter the Main Chapel, which is all bedecked in familiar celebratory décor of blue lights and bunting. Pictures of the Swami fill the room, his familiar orange robe and orange watch cap so recognizable. Pictures of his round face, his expression sometimes serious, sometimes light and engaging, can be seen in different spots throughout the building. But this is the first time in seventeen years that he is the center of attention and focus.

We find seats. I sit midway back from the altar, spaciously away from the presenters but near enough to see. I sit with Ras on my left, and our good friend, Andy, in a sacrilegiously bright blue T-shirt on my right.

I attempt to take a few breaths. My chest feels tight and unwilling to receive fresh energy. My palms are sweaty. *Wow*, I think. *This is not fun yet.*

There is a general hubbub of white-clad people excitedly milling about. Ras goes to mingle with these familiar faces from so long ago. I stay put and from my emotional observation deck, I watch. Familiar characters, same personalities as so long ago, some with gray hair now, dot the landscape of the Chapel. I feel surprised by my emotional distance from them, yet fully accepting of it. I watch Ras brightly chitchatting, aware, as usual, of our very different responses to life. I look to my right to Andy. He shrugs his shoulders, characteristically and kindly neutral.

I close my eyes for a few breaths and am effortlessly taken back to 1995. In a moment I am there. Sitting in this very room, with Ras on this very same left side of me, surrounded by the more senior ashram disciples, I return to the day that the guru's downfall became public:

Deep silence and anticipatory anxiety filled the air of the chapel. I could hardly breathe. We were seated in a giant circle filling the huge, high-ceilinged room. We wore white on that day, too. Rumors of upheaval and change had been wildly spreading for a few days. Ramanan, a senior disciple and member of the board of directors, looked pale as he stood before us. In his quiet yet commanding way he began talking. He cut to the chase: "Accusations of sexual impropriety against Gurudev have been made by several women."

Sobs filled the Chapel. Voices cried out things that my ears seemed unable to offer my brain.

He hesitated, looked around, and continued. "A team has been established to investigate these allegations."

Chaos emerged. As if a malevolent genie uncorked a riotous bottle of anarchy, all hell broke loose. Several people stood and shouted over one another. Our subdued and contained spiritual affect seemed forever changed.

I was terrified to the bone, unable to move.

Suddenly a tiny and tidy man named Sahil, whose deep disconnection in his eyes always concerned me—I'd never seen him make eye contact with anyone—dashed out of nowhere, madly running toward the altar. There the guru's chair sat with a large portrait of him in it. As usual, when Gurudev wasn't there, a large picture of him would mark the place. In one movement, maneuvering around Ramanan, Sahil lunged for the picture, grabbed it, and began slamming it against the chair! Glass exploded everywhere as the sobs intensified in the room. There was a blurred flurry of movement around Sahil as other folks tried to subdue him.

I thought of the phrase "cognitive dissonance."

It doesn't seem possible, I thought, *to have these different feelings at once*. I acknowledged to myself that I was simultaneously terrified, broken-hearted, and deeply and violently freezing.

The microphone startles me back into present time. I slide into this Sunday afternoon's moment. It is Varshana's voice that brings me back. She is the master of ceremonies for Bapuji's birthday celebration, a woman of much grounded maturity. Both her presence and her kind words of welcome relax me back into this present moment.

"Close your eyes," she says as she invites us into an opening meditation. "Allow the grace of this moment to enter you. Know that you are held in the arms of Bapuji's love now—and then—and always."

I am slightly touched, but manage to keep my emotions at bay.

Varshana introduces a young Indian woman, spry and crazily beautiful, to lead us in seated Indian dance. As we sit in our chairs, we practice the hand and arm movements she demonstrates for us. I feel embarrassed and self-conscious as I strive to get the movements right, knowing full well there is no right or wrong in this realm. Yet that overlay of striving for perfection is always available to me, if I choose it. It appears I am choosing it.

I look at Kari, a six-foot-two former disciple, wearing a gray New England Patriots sweatshirt. He sits a row in front of me and to my right, so I have a fine view of his seated dancing. He sways, he moves, he glides, his expression soft and gentle; a huge and giant man, he appears surrendered fully into this very feminine expression. He looks a lot more comfortable than I am in this moment, moving my hands back and forth.

I have a wave of remembrance of the dearness of the Kripalu men in the ashram; they always appeared so willing to participate in whatever was thrown to them, so out-of-any-gender-box.

I realize that the genuine gentleness of the Kripalu ashram men has been precious to me.

I feel a stab of missing in my heart. I suck the feelings in.

And so the afternoon unfolds. Each presenter offers tidbits of evocative stories about meeting Swami Kripalu, about his humor, his ferocious integrity, and his siddhas, his yogic powers. I manage to surf the waves of my own feelings without dipping into the water.

The presentations characteristically go on. And continue to go on.

The day is getting a little long, I think, craning my neck to see the clock on the wall behind me. *Just like us to run long-winded and late*, I grumble to myself. Realizing that Ras and I have two cars, knowing Ras will stay till the bitter end, I begin to consider leaving. The decision feels heavy and overwhelming. To leave . . . not to leave. I don't know how to decide.

I am saved by Varshana's announcing that the afternoon will end now with Arti.

Arti!

One of my favorite things in the ashram, Arti is a Hindu ritual in which light from wicks soaked in ghee (purified butter) is offered to one or more deities. We used it at the end of gatherings as a way to offer the day back, to offer the light back. Although I could only learn snatches of its Sanskrit words over the years—what a block I had—the familiar melody was hauntingly deep in me.

We all characteristically charge up toward the altar, to stand near the light. I move forward with Ras and Andy. No ghee wicks for us today. Since our visit from the Berkshire County Fire Warden a few years back, Kripalu is a wick-free, candle-free, and incense-free environment. We will use our politically correct, in-compliance, battery-operated candles to offer the light of grace to ourselves and back to Swami Kripalu. What irony—to practice an ancient ritual with battery-run candles—yet it's all good and sweet to my heart.

The harmonium player starts the so-familiar melody. The chanter begins the Sanskrit words. I find words I recognize and slide into voice. In and out, what I know, what I don't. Two senior former-disciples start waving the offering of light, their backs to us, to the large portrait of Swami Kripalu that has been reinstated for this event in the Main Hall. It is touching and yet I still manage to maintain my own emotional distance. The music begins to move me as I participate as best I can, swaying to the ancient rhythm.

The leaders turn, complete with offering the light to Bapuji. Now they begin to offer the light to us. The people around me extend their palms and their hands, to receive the blessings. I do the same mindlessly.

I feel the light blanketing over me in waves of grace.

Something so much bigger than my mind, for the first time this afternoon, is unleashed.

I feel the light wrapping me up, flooding over me in even more waves of grace.

Wave after wave of feelings cover me.

I am filled with a physical sense of overwhelming gratitude that completely saturates me now. Cellularly I am immersed in a river of gratefulness. I am wordless and thoughtless for a few powerful breaths. And then the words come:

For everything. For every single moment. I am blessed and grateful.
All that this path of Kripalu has given me. All of it. I am blessed.

And then a shift of feelings comes soaring up into me—the gratitude slides into a missing, a deep stabbing at the innards of my heart. I am choked with it. I am breathless within it. I am powerless over it.

A missing for what was, the collective sharing of spirituality, the shared rituals, the intended one-pointed and communal purpose. I could bend over and wail forever into the earth my missing of what was, the best of this crazy-wacky ashram.

And the moment passes.

And Arti ends.

And the afternoon is over.

I walk out of the Chapel, the buzzing sounds of people networking behind me.

I am flooded with the contradictions that are this path.

I head toward my office, then my car.

I fall into the rhythm of my life, paradox after paradox, step after step.

They are all true; they are all sacred.

They are all inevitable.

The whole world is one family. No matter what religion we are following, if we cannot love others then we are not following religion but the illusion of religion. Where there is no unity, no love, no harmony among each other, how can there be religion?

—Swami Kripalu

Questions for Your Heart

- Did you have an event in your life after which everything else was different? Consider.
- How were you impacted—in body, in mind, and in spirit?
- Have you ever attended a reunion of any sort—a family gathering—a gathering of friends—where you noticed contrasts between the past and the present? What feelings are evoked, as you reflect on the past? As you consider the present?
- What has changed in your life to allow you to acknowledge and affirm the value of the past?

 Practice for Your Life

Take a few deep breaths as you sit quietly. Consider: How can you acknowledge what used to be in your life, as a way to be more fully present with what is?

Just imagine.

9

And So It Is–Dogs, Babies, Daycare, and the Like

When you come to a fork in the road, take it.
—that famous yogi, Yoga Berra

Decisions once made live forever. And so it is. Or at least, that is how it seems in this moment.

I look in my rearview mirror. He is sitting up like a big boy, looking out the window with such curiosity and downright fascination. *Oh! He's so cute*, I think. *I love it when he tilts his head from side to side like that.*

The gray of early morning is streaked now with slices of pink, the sky opening organically and seamlessly into this new day's light. It is a clean and fresh moment, one of newness and possibility.

The road is comfortably clogged with morning traffic; folks scurrying to work, a school bus picking up kids bundled in multicolored parkas, a dented pickup truck with its snowplow ready for today's weather, and a mob of cars pulling off into the Dunkin Donuts drive-through for their morning jolt. I am happy to belong to the throng; happy to have a destination. I'm happy to be part of this morning procession toward something more than just my work.

I want something more than just my work right now. In this, my sixth decade, the never-ending work cycle is wearing thin. As much as my work has fed me, its stressors are accumulating. And so are their physical ramifications.

I look in the rearview mirror again and smile.

I never wanted a child. Perhaps that's not fully accurate. I might have wanted a child—like, the end result of someone else's effort. If someone had given me an eight-year-old little girl at some point, I might have positively responded. But I simply never wanted to make it happen. And life fully conspired at different ages of my development to support my myopic, age-specific perception of this choice-point.

For years, as a radical lesbian feminist (I think that was what I called myself), there was good reason to not imagine having a family. During my mid-twenties to mid-thirties, I was living in a womyn-centered world (sorry, we spelled it *womyn*, as to not repeat the word *man* in the middle of the word. Whatever. It seemed important then). Although a few of my feminist sisters had children, I was busy exploring myself, my expression as a *womyn*, as a lesbian, as a sexual being, as a self-perceived "radical." Having a child didn't exist in the realm of possibility. I needed my life to be more marginal, more removed from the habitual decisions made within the dominant culture. It was a decision not made during those wild and young New York City years that, in effect, made a decision. I was so profoundly self-centered and self-referenced; the option of sharing my life with a child was not on my radar of possibilities.

The car, my trusty Prius, feels steady beneath me, the two-lane road humming quietly along. My father's daughter, I love driving.

The next phase of my development centered on getting sober and clean. Life connived to thrust me into the river of self-development during my mid-thirties to mid-forties: *figure yourself out or die*, life essentially said to me. And it keeps on saying that, to this day, but in a quieter and more subtle voice. The journey of early sobriety demanded full focus then—at least the way I perceived it during those early years.

My morning musing is interrupted by some movement in the back seat. Zac Joseph is finding himself a more comfortable way of sitting, supporting himself in lying down and resting along this leg of our journey.

"I know," I say to my boy. "It is important to get comfortable along the way."

I smile as I put on the car's directional, turning left onto West Housatonic, a main thoroughfare for morning traffic in this town.

I'm amazed at how much I enjoy this once-a-week morning drive. Even though it is out of my way, about a fifteen-minute drive in the opposite direction from work, I savor the time, the newness of the morning, the driving, sharing of special time with Zac.

Twelve Step program talks about being "a worker among workers, one among many." Something about this morning drive connects me with a bigger world, offers me a bigger and more connected sense of myself. I am one among many, making my way, supporting the wellness of my family as the day begins.

"Almost there now," I say to the fellow in the back seat. He is remarkably patient, much more than I am in many circumstances.

My many years in the ashram were the third overlay of my life experience. No space or time existed to imagine anything but being present, serving, praying, and growing. There was no real individual expression. It was all for the greater good, which made complete sense at that moment of my world—my forties into my fifties.

So by the time I was emotionally and logistically ready, with a home and a partner, to realistically consider having a child, I was too old.

Funny. I didn't notice getting old. It just happened. I am almost mid-way through my sixties. And I wish more than life itself that I had an adult child to walk with me through these next years, these years of aging and letting go, these years of mystery and unknown.

We pull into the driveway. Zac gets up now, awakened into true happiness. The bigger-than-life sign announces that this is the home of *Love Us and Leave Us*, Zac's weekly doggie day care immersion. These are his people, his doggies. He adores it here.

I grab at his leash as he happily bounds out of the car. He is a medium-sized fellow at fifty-eight pounds, lean and strong, black and silver, with the long face of a Wolfhound marked by perfect Groucho Marx eyebrows that frame his soulful poet-eyes, his silver goatee simultaneously both pointed and disheveled. He eagerly pulls me toward the door, his entryway into a world I can never imagine, a world of boundless smells, playmates galore, wild runnings, deep restings; a pack, a tribe, a community of his peers.

Formerly a restaurant, the ex-bar frames the right wall, now displaying canine-related purchasing opportunities, delectable doggie snacks, and bright dog collars made of multicolored lanyard.

Renee opens the door to the right, to the inner sanctum, where we mere mortals/humanoids are forbidden to enter, for "insurance purposes" we are told.

She welcomes him passionately and seemingly sincerely. "Oh. Buddy. Buddy. Buddy. Zacy. Joey. Wolfie. Doodle."

He shimmies his way toward her, wiggling his delight at her mere presence on the planet, fully demonstrating one of his more descriptive nicknames, WiggleWorm. Renee smiles at me, a quick hello/goodbye, as they both disappear seamlessly into the room, without a backward glance from either canine or human. The door quickly closes behind them, keeping the other apparently rowdy dogs contained.

I stand alone in the hallway, feeling typically abandoned as I sometimes do at this moment of the process.

No need to acknowledge your mother, I think. *I'll pick you up this afternoon. I'll walk you this evening in the cold and ice. I'll do it again in the morning. And on and on.*

Yet as I stand alone in the hallway, I realize Zac's capacity to leave me so effortlessly has to be built on his trust for me. In that moment I am able to appreciate his full-bodied trusting of and embracing of life, two arenas in my world which are less developed than his.

I turn and head for the parking lot. As I step out into the brightening morning, a large, imposing silver pickup truck zooms in and parks next to my humbled, squat-looking Prius. In it are a tall man and a tall dog, sitting incredibly close together. I love the sight of a pickup truck, man-and-dog one in the front seat, betraying the butchiness of the vehicle, demonstrating their loving hearts.

This Dog and This Man exit the truck in one unit; both lope in long-legged strides toward the day care, Man extending his blue-jean-work-boot-long-legs to keep up with the leash-free, muscled brown retriever. As he passes me, Man turns his head. Our eyes meet. We smile at each other.

I open my car door, strangely emotional.

We are one; Prius and pickup, Man and Lesbian, local and transplant, one in our love of our canines, one in the circle of giving and receiving of love that is bestowed upon us by our animal companions.

Wow, I think. *Wow. The lessons Zac continues to teach me.*

I open the car door and get inside. I catch my breath, turn the car on, and back out of the lot, leaving doggie daycare behind me. At the main road, I put on my directional, look out at the flow of traffic, and turn right to join it.

It wasn't until my dad died that I began to feel the weight, the reality of being a childless woman, I think. That, of course, was hugely magnified when my mom died five years later.

I continue to muse:

After their deaths, support felt thinned out in my life; love felt finite. Without my parents' infinite presence and caring, no matter how intrusive that might have felt at earlier developmental moments, my world was inexorably and forever changed without them.

And without them standing between me and my mortality, the void, the mystery of aging has become real.

No adult child exists to walk with me through these next decades of unknown, as I head toward the Great Mystery.

This is my one and only regret of my lifetime.

I take a breath, finally bored with my heavy morning musings.

And so I practice with my animal companions. Their sped-up life cycles giving me opportunities to love and let go, to fully adore them and surrender to their shortened lives.

I take a breath, now fully done with my own thoughts. I consider the option of public radio, leaning toward the radio dial.

Turning it on, I surrender to the flow. I surrender to the airwaves of America.

There are two possible situations. One can either do this or do that. My honest opinion and friendly advice is this: do it or do not do it. You will regret both.

—Søren Kierkegaard

Questions for Your Heart

- Is there anything in your life that you regret doing? That you regret not doing?
- Are you able to see other situations in your life that emerged, because you did (or didn't) do this thing?
- Is it possible to get more comfortable with your decision? What would that look like?
- Is there anything in this story with which you identified?

 Practice for Your Life

Find a quiet spot. Get comfortable. Invite your spine to be upright and relax and soften your gaze.

As you sit, begin to watch your breath as it comes and goes. Notice the sounds around you. Feel the temperature of air on your hands and face.

From this place of silence, imagine that the concept "mistake" does not exist in your world.

Breathe out judgment of self.

Breathe in radical self-compassion.

As you watch the breath, empty out of self-negativity.

As you breathe in, fill yourself up with silent, boundless compassion for the choices you have made on the planet.

Practice.

10

Wild Thing—Lessons in Blood, Guts, and Surrender

I am subject to aging. Aging is unavoidable.
I am subject to illness. Illness is unavoidable.
I am subject to death. Death is unavoidable.
I will grow different and separate from all
that is dear and appealing to me.
—Buddhist Daily Reflections

He runs like the wind, light and loose and wild. He runs with full abandon. He runs as if gravity doesn't exist, leaping and thrashing and throwing himself through the air. As my mother would say, he runs like nobody's business.

He runs like a wild thing.

I adore him, with a love unabashed, a love unintended, a love so visceral that it surprises me as it flushes up into my throat, filling me with warmth.

I trudge up the dirt path laden down by my humanness, feet heavy in my hiking boots. He is off to my left, deep in the woods, dashing about, unencumbered by humanity. The cowbell on his collar identifies his location. Since he is in and out of sight, the ice-cream-truck-bell tinkles as our audio GPS.

Ras and Ann walk ahead, deep in conversation. I traipse up the hill of Kennedy Park, this late afternoon in fall, feeling sticky and still warm with the heat of this Indian summer day. I'm tired and cranky, *too much going on*, I mumble to nobody.

The bell softens, fades into silence. With it my heart quiets, slows, and stops. Ras handles his wildness with such aplomb. She trusts the process of his recall more; she simply has more faith in life than I. His wildness threatens the safety of my love for him. I want the illusion of him safe, at my side.

Silence. Long protracted silence. Ras doesn't seem to notice, as she continues walking and talking. My heart, from stillness, leaps up 100 mph and pounds its way into my throat.

Where is he? These silent moments of hiking with Zac are timeless, endless, one minute becoming an eternity, a few minutes hanging timeless in space.

A tiny tinkle emerges from our front left. Wild Boy, my Zac Joseph Doodle the Dog, bolts out ahead of us, a flash of black-silver, crossing the path, as if to say, *Hi, it's me*, and disappears again into the woods to my right. He is in his element. In a very real way, I am not. Hiking with him, which we do regularly, does not relax me. I am armed against natural disaster, against his potential injury, against his disappearance down a gully, never to return to my arms again. Simply said, I am an over-attached canine companion.

And we hike and we hike, so I am ongoingly confronted by his natural exuberance, his untamed freedom in the woods. He who cuddles up into me, leaning his sixty-pound body into my arms, collapsing into my lap; he who loves baby-talk and table scraps and soft stuffed animals to carry around—he who is my dear young man dog, he is also a wild animal, driven by scents and pulls unimaginable to my "developed" mind.

How can he be both, a cuddly domesticated living Muppet, while existing elementally as such a wild thing? I don't understand.

We continue. I traipse. Ras and Ann socialize. Lucy Doodle the Dog runs, plays, returns, runs forward again. Older, more people-orientated, less a hunter, she enjoys being in relationship with the people. Meanwhile Zac bolts hither and thither, left side and right—all over the map. He dances between elegant flowing grace and canine clumsiness.

We turn right toward the Pond. *The woods are beautiful*, I think. With the leaves falling, space emerges between the trees in which vistas surprisingly present themselves. The late afternoon sun is shifting, throwing long shadows through the trees. It is all quiet, an occasional jogger passing us. Do I feel a molecule of relaxation?

Halfway to the Pond, our turn-around point, Ann's words squeeze my heart: "I think Zac is bleeding." I look and sure enough there are bloody paw prints on the dirt. I know this moment. We have been here before, time and again. He slows his running and limps toward us. My entire being reacts with constricted breath, tightness of muscle.

"Oh, it's his leg," Ras says. We are experts at this. Our vet says Zac Joe, of all his canine patients, has received the most stitches from paw and leg cuts, perhaps a by-product of his uninhibited nature.

We gather around him and look more closely. What I see constricts any remaining breath out of me.

Blood is spurting out of Zac's back left leg. This is not just your normal, run-of-the-mill bleeding. This is rhythmic spurting.

We realize we are in trouble and huddle around him. A good twenty minute walk back to the car awaits us, and he is losing blood quickly. I can hardly breathe. I take off my flannel shirt and wrap it around his leg.

Do we make a tourniquet? How? We try wrapping the shirt on his leg and start moving, slowly back, retracing our tracks. Ann takes charge of Lucy, who becomes instantly irritated and upset, pulling and thrusting her way toward her brother.

I want a vet, any vet, here and now. Right here. Right now. There are none in the woods. This is bad.

Miracles swiftly unfold in the midst of this emotional chaos. I am both aware of the miracles and feel untouched by their grace:

> Miracle number one: I have my cell phone.
> Miracle number two: It is charged and we have reception.
> Miracle number three: It is Thursday early eve, the night our vet has office hours.
> Miracle number four: Directory information gets the vet's office on the phone since I'm too freaked to remember the number.

No, no tourniquet, the vet tech says. *Just use compression on it. And get him in to us. We'll be here waiting for him.*

Get him in to us.

We'll be waiting for him.

I wonder how our sixty-pound dog, spurting blood, will make it down the mountain to the car, with another twenty-minute drive to the office. I don't know.

Lucy continues to leap and pull toward him. Ann focuses on her, keeping her forward-moving.

Ras and I walk with Zachy. He is walking, slowly moving forward. He is too heavy to pick up for us, this sixty-pound boy—it's not even an option that enters my mind. He walks slowly and carefully, seemingly a little dazed. There is a lot of blood in our wake, on my hands, on the shirt.

We inch our way.

I have no idea how I am doing this. I am just—doing this. This is what is here to do. I find no prayers, no declarations of surrender in my heart or mind. I just see blood and feel—hollow terror.

A few joggers pass us unaware. It does not even occur to me to ask for help.

After interminable creeping forward, we somehow make it to the top of the hill, facing now the down-slope toward the parking lot. Out of my peripheral sight there is movement. A mountain bike. A woman. She stops and interrupts our intensifying private drama.

"Do you guys need help?"

Her words hang in the air. Words of grace. Words of an angel.

YES, we all agree. HELP.

WE NEED HELP.

She leans her upscale mountain bike against a tree and approaches us. Young, dark-haired, broad-shouldered, fit for the woods, she comes over and assesses this moment of our crisis.

I am not sure what happens now. There is a blur of movement, a blur of activity. She, this unknown savior, has lifted our sixty-pound dog over her shoulders, two legs, the bloody hind-leg facing me on the left, two more facing Ras on the right. She begins to walk, one considered step at a time, down the mountain. I am barely present enough to attempt to hold compression on the cut; Ras stabilizes his other side, while Ann and Lucy precede us.

I have a Jesus-Moment. I am a Jew; truly I don't know much of Jesus, now, then or ever. But I see an image flashing across my mind's eye—am I hallucinating?—of Jesus carrying a little lamb over his shoulders, just like this stranger is doing.

We inch our way down. Minutes pass. We exchange few words. She continues her considered walking, step by step. I ask her name.

Abigail.

Time passes. We inch. We creep. We move downward, Zac a bundle around her shoulders. I am sweaty and clammy and numb, all in the same moment. Time stops.

Eventually, we come to the level path, the mountain now behind us. A straight-away followed by a little hill lies ahead, behind which the parking lot awaits. We stumble our way forward, Abigail's face pinched with concentration.

Somehow I see the parking lot up ahead.

We make it. I almost allow myself a breath of relief. But no, now the next challenge emerges. There is no lasting relief to draw up. The end of one phase of this crisis simply merges into the next.

More blurry movement and actions—fuzzy decisions—Ann takes Lucy in one car as I am swept with Miracle number five: Ann is here to deal with Lucy, with her own car. Having Lucy to deal with would make this even more complicated. Abigail lifts Zachy into the back of the car, runs to the sporting goods store by the trail to get ice. Ras gets in the back with him. I put my hands on the wheel, trembling from inside out, trying to breathe. I turn the car on—it shudders with me. Abigail returns with ice, which Ras tries to hold onto his leg. We offer our stuttered thanks to this miracle mountain woman, this flesh embodiment of divine intervention. I wildly back the car out, screech, and right it toward the road.

It's dark now, and we are right smack in traffic. I get lost in my head—which way to go? Which way? There are several, too many, options. I decide on one—forge forward. Right into traffic, more traffic, into red lights, and second guessing. I do not relax. I do not surrender. I fight myself and this moment, cursing at my choice.

Ras struggles in the back with the ice, with the dog. At a red light I look back—pools of blood on our new, stain-protecting seat cover. (Miracle number six saves the car seat from ruin.)

It is a long, long twenty-minute ride. I speed, I jockey ahead of cars, I get stuck in the crawl of evening traffic. I do not relax at all. It simply gets harder. In retrospect I will feel badly about not dropping down into a more mindful, surrendered state—it doesn't happen. I am freaked and continue to self-accelerate my own chosen freak-dom.

Finally after an eternity of moments, unending heavy minutes, I screech into the vet's parking lot. Ras runs in to get them as I sit trembling at the wheel. Two of the techs, such good women, reach in and, in one movement, get Zac out of the car and carry him through the back door. I am aware of his bulk in their arms.

The end of this phase of the crisis just folds into the next. Now what?

Ras and I stumble into the waiting room, like near survivors of some unnamed bloodbath. We look at each other. She is pale, shaking her head, looking around. I eventually make my way to the bathroom.

Standing at the sink, I push up my shirt sleeves, baring my elbows. Both my forearms are covered in dry blood. I try to wash the blood off. I scrub and scrub and weep into the bloodied water. A thousand years later, at home that night, I will find blood on my bra, blood on my belly, blood on my sneakers and socks. Staring at the stranger in the mirror, I know that she will be forever tainted by this experience.

Miracles prevail over reality.

Zac spends that night at the vet's. We do not. Happy by this point to leave him behind, we make our way home to a trembling Lucy, falsely calming her and ourselves. Zac gets innumerable layers of stitches, does not need a transfusion (my internal veterinarian prescribed this protocol), comes home the next day with his pain medication, a fully wrapped leg, a cone to prevent his interference, and a steep bill. I want his pain medicine—I think I've earned it, but I refrain, drawing on breath and prayer for renewal.

It works out. He comes out of this better than we do.

We absorb the costs on all levels. Despite being fully shaken, we move forward.

Eventually Zac returns to his life of free wilding in the woods. His bell tinkles, quiets, tinkles again. I bear it. Time passes. He has some minimal cuts over the next months; nothing competes with the blood bath-from-hell, but all, nevertheless, carrying with them stitches, bills, and the dreaded cone.

We track down the mystery of Abigail, blessing her, gifting her, thanking her selflessness.

We continue.

Until Mother's Day. Nobody really knows what happened to him that day in the woods. The staff at Tufts Animal Hospital, one of the best in the country, a three-hour drive from our house that pouring rainy night, where he spends three days, eventually diagnoses his injuries as "blunt-force trauma." This means he probably ran full-Zac-speed into a rock or a tree.

His belly is covered with externalized lymph pockets, called *lymphoceles*, a condition unknown to canines. The medical staff is interested enough in his condition to consider writing a paper on him. His "team" of doctors gives him a ninety-minute MRI to trace the leaking lymph fluid. No source is found and after thousands (yes, thousands) of dollars' worth of tests and care, he is sent home with bed rest and the directive to "watch his breathing."

Watch? Watch his breathing? My eyes do not leave his chest. I am riveted to his body, locked onto his every breath. Completely certain that he will die this time, I am again wrong.

Post-trauma, we talk to Dr. Mike, our home vet, a smart and sensible guy, who practices a great balance between allopathic science and radical common sense. His words shock me.

"Keep him on lead. Zac is not a candidate for off-leash walking. He is too lean—has no padding—and is 'a nut' in the woods. Keep him on lead."

My eyes zoom to Ras's. Really? This so violates the pledge we took for both our canine companions: YOU ARE A DOG. YOU GET TO LIVE THE LIFE OF A DOG, INCLUDING FREE RANGING IN THE WOODS.

I giggle nervously. Are we off the hook, never to worry again about his disappearance or the next bloodbath?

We talk and talk—process and process. Finally we agree. Zac Joseph Doodle will no longer run loose in the woods. We do not, neither financially nor emotionally, have the reserve for another catastrophe in us. He will walk on lead, have our fenced-in yard in which to party, and enjoy day care freedom and fancy once per week.

Relief and guilt compete inside my belly.

Time passes. Our hiking paradigm changes. Now Lucy is off leash, solo alpha girl in delight, while Zac stays with me on the expandable leash.

More time passes.

It is another beautiful Indian summer afternoon. We walk through Kennedy Park. Lucy runs and dashes, returning to our side, looking for fun. Zac, on his expandable leash, navigates his way, comes and goes, both tethered to me while fully exploring his circumference of freedom.

I wonder to myself:

Are we stewarding his safety? Or are we inhibiting his expression? Am I playing to my fears and supporting them, rather than growing forward into a new muscle of surrender?

I don't know. My feelings about this change inside me, morphing and shifting. Always morphing and shifting.

I call his name.

"Zac?"

He swivels his head around and looks—his long snout, his silvery beard, his black and silver fuzzy head—interested. Characteristically he tilts his head one way, then another.

"Zac? Are you good with this? We're doing our best."

His soulful, ancient brown eyes pierce through me, connecting, considering, pondering.

Then a sound interrupts; then movement darts to our left. His attention stolen, Zac wheels his head around, seeking the squirrel, always seeking the squirrel, as he slides through the door of Mystery, so close to me yet so very, very far away.

Live as if you were to die tomorrow.

—Mahatma Ghandi

Questions for Your Heart

- Have you noticed, in the midst of calamity, grace and support operating? When? How?
- Have you made a hard decision in your life in which you are torn?
- What gets you through emergencies? How do you deal?
- Does humor help you relax? How? Can you utilize this tool more?

 Practice for Your Life

Settle into a comfortable seated position. Practice elongating your spine, extending upwards from your sitting bones, right through the crown of your head. Relax into the extension, breathing deeply and slowly. Notice the breath as it comes and as it goes.

From this place of stillness, imagine the breath taking you more deeply inside. Fall back safely into the arms of breath and return even more deeply, more closely to yourself. Let each breath be the opening of a deeper and more precious doorway.

From this place of home, ask your heart to effortlessly create a prayer of acceptance, a prayer of surrender into reality. Receive the words, rather than forcing them. Allow these words, these prayers to be placed on the altar of your heart, without doing a thing.

And know that a prayer once given energetically lives forever. Let this prayer be an energetic beacon to guide you forward.

11

Lucy: A Love Story

Dogs are better than human beings
because they know but do not tell.
—Emily Dickinson

She is seventy-seven, short and blonde. Her self-esteem is larger than North America. It always was. When she was young, she was a wild and crazy thing, sowing her wild oats, with the heart of an athlete, both active and affectionate on her terms. She has slowed down recently, but she continues to see herself as the life of the party and lives fully into that role.

She is one of my greatest teachers.

Lucy.

She sits next to me, smelling like a combination of rotten eggs and wet fur. She is a canine Muppet-look-alike and one of the best friends I have ever had.

When I was fifty-three years old, eleven years ago, Lucy Doodle entered my life as my first dog companion. Little did I know, a friend and teacher lived inside that furry exterior.

Playing with my new iPhone, I hit the video button. I focus on her great face, long and white now with the years; her Albert

Einstein hair poking every which way, creating out-of-control haloes around her head, her beard straggly and pointy. I begin rolling the camera, pressing what I think might be the play button.

"Lucy, do something."

Uncharacteristically she sits stock still. Is she even breathing?

"Lucy—be cute. Do something."

Not a nano-movement, not even a slight tip of the head. Just those big eyes looking at me, opened and wider than the entryway to heaven, saying in her silent way:

"Why? Why would I move? There's no need to move. I am perfectly beyond-perfect the way I am. If you need movement, then you *move!"*

She cracks me up—I snicker and stop the video of the immobile dog.

I wasn't always able to laugh so freely at her. There were many years when I interpreted her independence, her strong-willed ways as a failure to my parenting efforts. If I were a better parent, a better trainer, she would have listened to the teacher in her Obedience One class rather than frantically barking at her seemingly attentive classmates. She would not have stolen the cocker spaniel's squeaky toy and caused pandemonium in the middle of the "sit" lesson. She surely would not have chomped freely on the little Bichon Frise's tail in Puppy Kindergarten. She certainly would not have pranced so happily down the road with the discarded beer can in her mouth, refusing to relinquish it. And of course, she would not have chewed the leash, playing the let's-go-this-way-and-not-that-way game while nibbling on her lead. For years.

The problem in our relationship was: it was all about me. I couldn't see her through my own self-centered fear. Lucy's fully self-expressed freedom reflected my own anal-retentive nature in strong relief. I was committed to the illusion of control over my life. I tried to extend that to Lucy, to no avail. Lucy Doodle pushed that edge over and over again. And upon that edge, I have grown.

We call it "The Red Zone." It was behavior that ran rampant in her earlier years, now only occasionally rearing its ugly head. One knows when Lucy is in The Red Zone by first looking at her eyes. If you look carefully enough, I swear, you can see her eyeballs spinning, each in opposite directions, like some cartoon depiction of a madman escaped from an asylum. Watch carefully; the eyes, usually wide and bright, begin to squint down into tiny pinpricks. Then, look to her gait, as it becomes a bouncy dance, with Lucy wildly pogo-sticking around you with impunity. And finally, listen for the Freshy Bark. This term is taken from my grandmother's frequent use of the word "freshy," meaning one who is a wise-cracker. Lucy offers her Freshy Bark, announcing to you that she is going to do It (whatever the It might be) in her own special way, completely separate from the requests of the people.

Rewind a decade or so. Lucy Doodle and I are on a solo walk, her other mom being at the gym. Lucy was trained to be off leash, with relatively successful recall, when she chose to return. We were hiking above the pond near our house, in the Boy's Club Camp property. We had a nice autumn walk; everyone, canine and human, was compatible. The day was cool; the trees were changing color, offering tinges of red and yellow streaking the blue sky. All was well. And then the time for our departure arrived. The mood changed.

As much as I requested, drawing from all of my training from our Obedience One classes (repeated twice) and from Obedience Two, Lucy would not return to me.

There was no obedience.

I held up the leash. I was firm in my command. "Come."

I became the strong and calm alpha dog.

I encouraged her with the lure of treaties.

All to no avail.

She continued her hop-scotching dance all around me, so close yet so far away. She barked, she hopped. She squinted. She pogo-sticked.

She didn't just ignore me. No, over time her ignoring morphed into open canine defiance.

I was initially furious. Then frustrated. Then—desperate.

Time passed; the sun was setting. In sheer desperation I laid out a trail of treaties—her Achilles Heel, the lure of food—a long, skinny trail of treats, from her to me. *This will work*, I thought, with desperation. Unfortunately like a master safe-cracker she skillfully snatched up each treat, avoiding capture as I lunged toward her fleeing blond body.

I pleaded. I implored.

I got on the ground and sobbed. I prayed. I begged.

I beseeched.

Nothing. No canine response.

While all the time, she Red Zoned it, dancing, barking, carrying on.

Cell phones had not made their way into our lives yet. I was stuck in the woods with a maniac dog.

I devised a plan; certainly I was smarter than she was, right? My car was parked at the bottom of the hill. Ras would have to drive right by it as she returned from the gym. I had full view of the road. I watched; I waited. This was the only hope I had.

The crazy canine carried on with her attraction/aversion dance, running close to me, then wildly dashing away.

Finally, Ras's gray car came snaking rounded the bend. I saw it! It was a miracle. I stood at the top of the hill, wildly waving my arms above my head, as frantic as the dog was by now. If I'd had a flare, I would have shot it into the Berkshire skies for rescue purposes.

Ras's car slowed and stopped.

My eyes couldn't believe it. There *was* grace! I was going to be rescued, not destined to spend a night in the cold Berkshire woods with a zealot dog committed to partying, who would probably leave me alone while she hooked up with whatever wolf pack was having the most fun.

Ras got out of the car and started walking up the hill toward us. Lucy shot like a bat out of hell past me, running wildly down the hill and literally flinging herself into Rasmani's arms, happy, I am certain, to be away from the wacky humanoid.

In the car, I fumed. I sobbed. I implored. I declared—I would never, NEVER walk alone with her again. I would never, NEVER endure her horrid behavior. I was committed to ignoring her, committed to never, NEVER liking her again.

Of course, I outlived these feelings. She was too cute to withstand. My heart softened beneath her fluffy blondness, her giant eyes, her endearing and piercing gaze—again and again, I fell in love with her. I realized, however, that something needed to shift in our relationship.

All of this led Lucy and me eventually to take counsel from the Bad-Dog Trainer of Berkshire County. We, as a family, continued to attend the Good-Dog Trainer classes. But Lois, the Bad-Dog Trainer, had the reputation for whipping even the most delinquent dogs in the county into shape. I was back on board for full participation in Lucy's training.

She and I went alone, since this issue seemed to be "about us." We wove our way through unfamiliar roads of South County, finding Lois's sprawling farm. Lucy was over-eager to meet Lois—or anybody, for that matter—and to find the next party, hopping out of the car as the party-girl I knew the delinquent canine to be. *This will teach her*, I vowed. *Some serious training for the incorrigible canine.* I felt smug in my hopefulness. We, the people, could outsmart her.

Lois met us at the barn. She was grim and dour, her affect matching her tan and stained-from-wear barn coat. *Not a big personality here*, I thought, with some judgment. Her face was lined and serious as she put Lucy and me through our paces.

We walked on leash.

We did *sit*.

We did *stay*.

We walked around the property, all the while Lois silently assessing the Delinquent Dog's misbehavior. Finally, despite my anxiety, our thirty-minute session came to an end.

"Yep," she flatly offered.

"Yep." Long pregnant pause. "It's pretty classic. You are trying to shield her from experience. You are trying to protect her and control her intake of life. It's not working. She is a fully alive puppy."

What? Why am I being psychoanalyzed? This is about Lucy, I thought, annoyed.

"Okay," she continued, to my dismay. "Your homework assignment is this: twice a week, take her into town. Take her right into the busiest part of town. Take her to the post office. Stand outside. Let her greet people. Let her look around. Practice allowing her to be who she is, in the midst of stimulation."

What?

"Your job," she concluded, "is not to keep her from life. Your job is to take her into it, and to teach her to listen to you, in the midst of what is happening."

So ended our session. I drove home with Lucy in the back seat, seemingly proud of herself.

I was fuming.

Take her into town? I wanted to lock her in the bedroom, without access to the outside world, in order to keep her safe. I felt embarrassed and annoyed.

However, over time and practice, Lois's approach proved to be right. Controlling her intake of reality—not unlike how I lived my own life—was not a sustainable strategy for a puppy. The Party Girl needed life and fun and interaction.

She taught me that I needed those things, too.

And endless Lucy-Lessons continued over the years. I am a better, more alive woman because of her presence and influence in my life.

But it is not about the past that I wish to speak. It is about the Now, the current lesson that Lucy, my friend/teacher is currently bringing me.

I look at her as she sleeps by my feet. She is eleven years old, slower now, with more white hair, more demanding in her demeanor, yet more relational, cuddlier than in her younger years. Her back hips bother her, limiting the speed and velocity of her running. She sleeps more than she plays these days. My heart catches, tightening into fear, as I consider her aging.

I don't want her to ever die. I don't want her to ever leave us. I adore her and need her. And yet I know that she is a being who is living an accelerated life cycle, growing into her final time on this planet. Because my dad was always going to die, from my early childhood on (cosmic joke: he lived to be eighty-four), terror of illness and dying continues to hold a strong emotional charge for me.

I think, with a smile, of Tillie, my mother, and of her final years. For some blessed reason, as she found herself after my father's death, I was able to find her in different and deeper ways. I had outlived whatever issues blocked me from loving her fully. Through the work I had done both emotionally, therapeutically, and spiritually, I was able to be with her and because of that being, I was given one of the most profound gifts of my life.

As I sit with Lucy, I'm swept with the simple memories of being with my mom that last year or so of her life:

- Playing Scrabble—she always beat the heck out of me, laying down simple, foundational words with silent and sometimes infuriating practicality.
- Sitting on her couch—laughing with *Dancing with the Stars*. She initiated me into and was fully responsible for my addiction to that show.
- Eating a simple meal—she ate so much less and cooked so much more simply. A hard-boiled egg, a piece of Melba toast, a slice of tomato—who knew food that simple could be so satisfying when shared with a quieter, slower love.

And I stayed with her, as she prepared to leave. I was able, in an imperfect way, to be of use to her, to be helpful, I do believe. My support was of an emotional nature, checking in regularly, asking about the books she was currently reading, talking about her day. Although in the moment, it didn't seem as valuable as the more practical and logistical support my sister offered her, I know today that each of our contributions made the perfect container to support my mother's journey.

When we moved her to Hospice that last month or so of her life, I watched her tears of anguish, so fully cognizant was she, so concerned about my niece's upcoming wedding. "Shiva before the wedding, *oye*," she said, breaking my heart.

But I was there for it. I received her angst. I witnessed her transition.

And I was there for her final breath. Taking my next breath without her, the first time in my fifty-seven years that I breathed without her on the planet, I was broken open. My shattered heart opened me up to the adult that I am today, the adult I really couldn't be with her still living.

And so I choose to be there for my Lucy Doodle, as she goes through her final time. I choose to:

- Pick up the damn ball whenever she drops it at my feet, no matter how important the human task at hand seems to be. What could be more important than throwing that ball down the hallway? As best as I can, I choose to fully and wholeheartedly play with her.
- Cuddle fully when the Blondie leans into when I'm meditating or couch-sitting.
- Be more lenient with her demands for treats. She clearly adores eating. I choose to honor her needs more, with less rigidity.
- Make the best decisions about her care that are possible.
- Love her and not leave her, until she needs to leave me.

The Buddhists say it well in their Four Daily Reflections:

I am subject to aging. Aging is unavoidable.

I am subject to illness. Illness is unavoidable.

I am subject to death. Death is unavoidable.

I will grow different and separate from all that is dear and appealing to me.

I choose to accept her aging process as best I can. I choose to love the heck out of her, to play with her, to cuddle with her, to snuggle with her, to steward her life on the planet as best as possible. I choose to notice my fear and ignore it, continuing to know Lucy more deeply, more intimately, and more fully.

I choose to keep my entire being open to my friend/teacher, the wacky, the wonderful, the Lucy Doodle of my heart. I choose to allow her to continue to love me and to teach me, until her final breath.

And well past that, too. Of this I am certain.

Bazougey
Where goes he now, that dark little dog,
    Who used to come down the road barking and shining?
He's gone now, from the world of particulars,
    the singular, the visible.

So, that deepest sting: sorrow. Still,
    is he gone from us entirely, or he
a part of that other world, everywhere?

Come with me into the woods where spring is
    advancing, as it does, no matter what,
not being singular or particular, but one
    of the forever gifts, and certainly visible.

See how the violets are opening, and the leaves
    unfolding, the streams gleaming and the birds
    singing. What does it make you think of?
His shining curls, his honest eyes, his
    beautiful barking.
                    —Mary Oliver, from the upcoming *Dog Songs*
                        (with permission from the author)

Questions for Your Heart

- Have you been in a relationship in which you were not able to see the other clearly?
- What blocked you from seeing?
- Have you noticed how trying to control another person or a situation might be a way to keep yourself comfortable?
- Are you aware of letting go in relationship with others? What does this look like?

 Practice for Your Life

Repeat this mantra aloud. Imagine it echoing within you:

As best as I can, I'll be with my self. And from my self, I will be with you.

If this speaks to you, bring it consistently into your life. Speak it upon awakening; walk with it as it becomes alive in you. Remember, repetition offers consistency; consistency opens the doorway to solace.

12

Once, Twice, Three Times a (Married) Lady

The minute I heard my first love story
I started looking for you, not knowing
how blind that was.
Lovers don't finally meet somewhere.
They're in each other all along.

—Rumi

I wish I could zoom back in time and address my eight-year-old self. She was so cute, that Little Nan, so terrified about how she wanted to kiss the girls and not the boys, already so hidden, so lost to herself. I see her wearing widely cuffed blue jeans, black high-top sneakers (an insecure fashion icon well before her time), a faded, striped T-shirt that held her slightly protruding belly, and some sort of headgear. She was big on headgear. In this retrospective, she is probably wearing her white yachting cap, its brim shading her eyes from the afternoon sun. She holds her long plastic spyglass against her leg—one never knows when one might need a spyglass.

I long to tell her, "Honey, it's going to be all right. Your life will suck for a long time, and then it will get much, much better. You are even going to have a wife someday. Hang in there."

What a radical and healing offering that might have been to that little girl, already so disguised to herself as a child. A wife? How absurd and ridiculous. Only men with penises get wives, everybody knows that. Hence having a penis seemed like a darn good idea, since it seemed to assure one a wife. Ah, here was something else to be ashamed about, the longing for a penis, a secret that traveled with me well into my early lesbian-feminist days.

Wait . . . a wife? That option simply did not exist for me; it did not occur on my radar screen of life possibilities. I was a woman. *Even if I love other women, I don't get a wife. Not in this lifetime, anyway.*

My first dip into matrimony begins many years ago, with the first woman I ever loved acting as a powerful catalyst. She was a Filipina whom I met during my Peace Corps stint on her island of Mindanao. After many months, the intensity of loving her freaked me out so thoroughly that I eventually had to leave her and the dust, the heat, the craziness of that country behind. I came home and married a man. It made twisted yet perfect sense. Surely there existed no way to be with her, my Filipina lover. She lived about 9,000 miles away and, even if she lived next door, the option to be with her didn't exist on Planet Earth. At least it didn't exist on *my* Planet Earth. I was home, back in Pennsylvania with my parents. I knew what I had to do.

The year was 1972. He was my former college "boyfriend," a simpatico and nice-enough guy, a completely sexually-non-threatening fellow. I had fully and forever broken up with him upon my college graduation, knowing, in spite of what we shared in common—a love of movies, writing, and marijuana, not necessarily in that order—that I didn't like him very much.

Post Peace Corps, recovering from reverse culture shock, a broken heart, and the biggest hemorrhoid imaginable, I stood in my parents' kitchen, next to the washer and dryer of my childhood. Picking up the corded phone, I dialed his number. Waiting for him to pick up, I listened to the echoes of the ring. Inside of me a voice of deep resignation chimed in, "It's okay. I can make this work."

So we got married that summer. I was not there to make that decision. The decision was made for me, molded by external circumstances and cultural expectations. I was a nice Jewish girl, on the nice Jewish girl choo-choo train. Marriage to a man was the next stop. It literally didn't matter that I did not like him. The poor man was my cover, something for which I will be forever sorry.

And of course, it didn't work.

After Marriage #1 and its subsequent divorce, decades unfolded filled with the subsequent dramas of: coming out as a radical lesbian-feminist in the heady air of the 1970s New York City, wild and senseless addiction, eventual and God-given sobriety, and my volunteering in a yoga ashram in Western Massachusetts.

I return to the theme of marriage—my first marriage to a woman. A visit from my now-friend, my then-acquaintance, Moose, opened the door to Matrimony #2.

The year was 1995. I had been happily and successfully living in the Kripalu ashram since 1989, growing and grooving and gaining insight into myself. In the fall of that year, however, our sheltered ashram existence was radically and forever interrupted. Our guru took a massive and public fall from grace as allegations of his sexual and financial misconduct were revealed. Circumstances unfolded with painfully traumatic, slow-motioned timing. More allegations were unearthed, until finally the guru was asked by the Board of Directors to leave the community he founded. Our vowed community, successfully based on volunteerism for decades, was shifting.

For most of the community's existence, heterosexual relationships were subtly discouraged; same-sex relationships did not exist. How I found home in a place so diametrically opposite from my lesbian-feminist roots, I will never understand. When I initially settled into Kripalu, my radical lesbian-feminist friends were aghast. How could I be in a place where such homophobia existed?, they demanded. One friend, when hearing about our ceremony of honoring the guru's feet, screeched over the phone at me, "You kissed his holy lotus *what*? How could that possibly work for you?"

I didn't know the answer—I just knew it was working.

But as the community shifted, so, too, the restrictions against same-sex relationship within the community were also shifting and releasing. In the midst of such a traumatic time, positive new changes began to slowly emerge.

One shift of paradigm that greatly impacted me was Kripalu's relationship-training track program for residents. Ashram residents with more than four years residency were eligible to participate in its relationships program—men with men, women with women for stages one through two. Facilitated by married, long-term residents, the program was a thoughtful exploration of mindful, spiritual, growth-producing relationship. Focusing on communication skills, tools for growth in relationship, the first two six-month sessions were helpful to me. I completed stages one and two before the fall of the guru.

At that point, I was so fully in love with my best friend, Rasmani, that I was quite the emotional and blubbering mess. She, having never been in relationship with a woman, had the luxury of falling in love with me and not actually knowing it. We spent wonderful and rich time together, swimming, hiking, biking, and talking, all the while my heart opening more deeply toward her. During Stages One and Two of the Relationships Program, she was unaware of my interest in her. I was committed to "holding the posture," allowing the relationship to develop without the intervention of my ego. This became a powerful spiritual practice for me, being open to feelings and letting go of the outcome I wanted.

Spring came. We went for a walk one morning and I spoke my truth to her as the sun was rising behind her. She looked bewildered, confused, shocked, and then, opened. The sun rose in her belly, too.

We decided to "explore relationship" by entering the yet-to-be-inhabited-by-a-gay-person Stage Three of the relationships program. We were on new ground. With the guru gone, we could move forward where no gay couple had been before us. The absence of the guru had made this possible. We had a fabulous mentor, Mimi, one of the senior former disciples, and her profound counseling and support helped us to strengthen our connection. I was happy and fully content with things the way they were, deeply knowing that nothing else could or should develop between us.

And yet the universe had another idea.

And then—enter Moose, Mr. Wildcard.

Moose—senior ashram resident, pillar of the community, jack-of-all-trades—a man loved and trusted by all. His seniority inhibited me; I knew him only from afar. At this moment in time, he was coordinating housing needs. Housing was a big deal at Kripalu, because little of it was decent. The system was built on seniority, single rooms were highly coveted, and shenanigans were known to unfold in housing placement.

I had my own single room by now, inhabited by me and my cockatiel, Buzz the Bird. We were reading one quiet Sunday afternoon when she and I were interrupted by a knock on the door.

Surprisingly it was Moose. Wearing a flannel shirt and well-used jeans, he was a big and hulky guy with soft eyes and a kind smile. I felt instantly embarrassed, since I really didn't know him yet respected him greatly from a distance.

"Hey, Aruni."

"Moose. Hi."

"I just wanted to mention to ya. I'm working on some room changes since so many people are leaving. By the way, married couples have first priority. There's that great suite of rooms on the third floor, ya know the one?"

What was this about? I nodded with obvious confusion.

"I'm just sayin'," he continued, "If you and Rasmani were married, you could have those rooms together."

I was shocked! If we were—married?

"I'm just saying," he finished, nodded knowingly, and turned to walk down the empty hall.

If we were married?

WTF . . . .

IF WE WERE MARRIED.

Light bulbs exploded in my head. Fireworks crashed overhead.

IF WE WERE MARRIED!

It never dawned on me until this moment—I could ask Ras to marry me!

And ask her I did, that next day, on my knee in her tiny room (soon to become a suite of rooms, I hoped and prayed).

She again looked startled, sitting on her bed looking down at me.

"Married?" she said.

I nodded earnestly, owning it as fully as I could as my idea.

"Well," she said, "I'm not saying no."

SHE'S NOT SAYING NO! I tap-danced down the hall. SHE'S NOT SAYING NO!

She didn't say no. Matrimony #2 was on its way toward me.

And on June 3, 1995, I was given the gift of an illegal, unsanctioned wife in a powerfully sanctioned way. Ras and I had our initial "marriage" ceremony with our Kripalu community, honoring our official-union-in-the-eyes-of-God-and-community, obviously unofficial in the eyes of many and the courts of the world. It was a blowout celebration for all, the beginning of healing the injuries that the Kripalu world endured by living within the shadow of its subtle internalized homophobia.

Ras and I happened to be the first couple to walk through the door of that emerging freedom. It was a heady and empowering celebration, a collective releasing of restriction that emitted joyful possibility for all.

The impetus for this, my second marriage, was delivered by a 200-pound Cupid with a flannel shirt and twinkling eyes.

During this time, change was in the air for me, in many ways. Living as a couple, sharing my life with someone on a realistic rather than a mere romantic basis, rebalancing my relationship to Kripalu as an employee rather than a spiritual disciple, renting a house in the area and commuting to work, getting a regular pay-check again—all of these things were destabilizing yet delicious opportunities to grow into this next phase of my life. And grow I did, into and through this next decade.

Time passed.

Almost an entire decade unfolded.

The shift in legal status for gay couples in the commonwealth of Massachusetts loomed on the horizon—even its mere possi-bility was beyond extraordinary. As the legislature continued its debate leading up to the vote, I followed the proceedings with bated breath. Would it really happen? Only five other places on the planet sanctioned gay marriage at that time—on the entire planet!—Quebec, the Netherlands, Belgium, Ontario, and Brit-ish Columbia. If it happened, Massachusetts would be the first state to offer marriage licenses to same-sex couples. And I lived in Massachusetts!

I eyed the political gay rights struggle in Boston anxiously. Would it happen? Would it pass? And it did! The world around me seemed to instantly and radically change, while remaining completely the same. Evolving from this upheaval, my official marriage proposal to Rasmani sounded more like an insistent whine than a plea of love. I was surely more adamant than romantic.

What was going on for me? What was the urgency, the push, to marry?

Time was limited, I was astutely and politically positive. I was sure that somehow the legal decision would be overturned by the Bad Guys in Boston. Rather than waiting until June 3, to sync up with our other, 1995 anniversary, I urged us to get married as soon as possible, on May 20—a few days past the law change.

What were the emotional layers that cannonballed me toward Matrimony #3?

My first layer was propelled by a generic, "Fuck you, America." The rebel, the radical feminist in me, released her initial layer of anger. "Fuck you, it's my right, too, you bastards." Justifiably righteous and indignantly angry, I was going to jump on board Matrimony #3, no matter what. Get outta my way!

And that was true enough. Yet beneath that, as I peeled away the anger, there existed a clearer, quieter response, a stepping into the righting of an injustice, the denying of civil rights. I, too, was guaranteed this liberty, this freedom of matrimony. Stepping forward into it was so awe-inspiring, so humbling that I could hardly breathe into my feelings about it.

And certainly my love for and commitment to Ras had to be part of my wild proposal. Yet, as in 1995, I really couldn't imagine our commitment to each other needing any further dedication or validation. How could a law or another ceremony change anything? I was wrong about that twice, both in 1995 and 2004. Again, standing before a few friends and speaking vows, in the little pagoda behind Anne and Thom's house, asking to be held accountable for those vows, offered a powerful deepening of our love and our lives together.

Perhaps most importantly, I made the clear and conscious decision to legally marry for the child, the little girl with the rolled-up jeans, the high-top sneakers, the yachting cap jauntily angled on her head. That little girl who hid her longings and her true self so well, that little girl who was afraid that even a look might betray her, that little girl who feared for her life—she could now come out of hiding.

I can see her now. She is standing on the lawn of her childhood house, looking out toward the blue-green of imaginary seas. She pulls her cap down more closely, in order to shade the sun. Lifting the spyglass, she scans the oceans, looking for pirates and the Bad Guys. She looks and looks.

There will be many seas she will have to cross, many waves she will have to ride. She will surely encounter pirates and even Bad Guys. But she will do it. And, through the grace of the bluest-of-blue states, Massachusetts, she will ride those oceans toward an awaiting wife.

May all of the wounded children within us have the healing opportunity to come out, to see and to be seen!

I would love to kiss you.
The price of kissing is your life.

Now my loving is running toward my life shouting,
What a bargain, let's buy it.

—Rumi

Questions for Your Heart

- As a child, what parts of yourself did you have to hide?
- Can you imagine: what might that child want to tell you? Receive that communication.
- As the adult you are today, what words of wisdom, comfort, or prayer would you offer directly to this child?
- Are you able to do something you never thought you could? Have you become someone you never imagined?

 Practice for Your Life

Offer yourself the gift of this mantra:

May you receive the blessings of your life.

May the people in your thoughts receive the blessings of your life.

May the people you meet receive the blessings of your life.

May the people you work with receive the blessings of your life.

May your family receive the blessings of your life.

May the people you love receive the blessings of your life.

May the people you do not love receive the blessings of your life.

May all beings receive the blessings of your life.

May you receive the blessings of your life.

Aruni Nan Futuronsky

Writer, teacher, and mindfulness coach, Aruni Nan Futuronsky finds life is best experienced with compassion, gratitude, and a whole lot of humor. She lives in Western Massachusetts with her wife, Ras, and canine teachers, Lucy Kay Doodle and Zac Joseph Doodle. A dynamic guide on the path of healing for body, mind, and spirit, Aruni is the creator of the innovative CD, *Life-Works, Meditations for Mindful Living*, and the author of two books, *Recovering My Voice: A Memoir of Chaos, Spirituality, and Hope* and *Already Home: Stories of a Seeker*.

CPSIA information can be obtained
at www.ICGtesting.com
Printed in the USA
BVHW070906090119
537368BV00009B/16/P